the hand embroidered haven

20 home sewing projects
with hand embroidery,
twilling & appliqué

Megan Frock

KP CRAFT
Cincinnati, Ohio

Contents

Introduction. 4

Getting Started. 6

Basic Stitches and Techniques. 8

1

**Living It Up
and Dining In**. 14

Static dish towel 16

Stacked framed art 20

Wreath of Roses pillow. 24

The Stump stool 30

Corner Crescent tablecloth 34

2

**Treat Me Sweet
and Put Me to Bed** 38

Urban Diamonds master quilt 40

Morning Roses robe 48

Mr. Deer and Dearest Deer travel cases 52

Seed Stitched shams 58

Scribbles laundry tote. 62

Itty Bitty Bedroom

Itty Bitty Bedroom 68

Balanced Baby crib quilt 70

Foxy Clock and Bunny Tube framed art 76

Catching Dreams crib mobile 82

Patched In boy's pants 86

Fawnsie Friendship little girl's dress 90

Big Kid's Crib

Big Kid's Crib 94

Jams twin quilt 96

Tellin' Time activity pillow 104

Electro Slide mini robe 110

Right Way napping bed 114

Call Me Sketch art backpack 118

Index 125

About the author 127

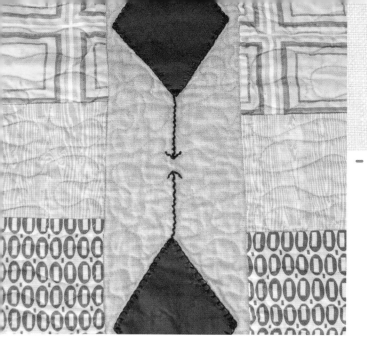

Introduction

Hand stitching is a skill that feels like home.

Knowing someone's hands have touched every morsel of a project warms my heart.

I can associate a memory with almost every project I have made. Maybe I was comfy on the couch watching a movie with my loved ones or in my studio chair with a cat curled up in my lap. Wherever it was, there are memories.

A project starts with a person in mind: You choose colors they will like, you think of them while you stitch, you wrap it with wishes and hope they will love it as much as you. As time passes, you see it in their home; you remember making it, they remember receiving it. It's really a cycle of love and appreciation—an appreciation for hand stitching, for giving your time and for sharing. Moreover, hand stitching is an art and a skill that should be practiced regularly and passed on so that future generations can reminisce about the past and plan for the future.

Embroidery doesn't have to be outdated, and you don't have to be a traditional gal. I'm not exactly the face of handwork; I've got a thing for tattoos, nose rings and stilettos. I take my sewing everywhere. Whether it's to the laundromat or the doctor's office, onlookers seem to be confused by my chosen hobby. "I didn't know people still did that," they say. "Why wouldn't you do this?" I respond. I want to shout, "Do you know how awesome this is?" It really is awesome and relaxing and fun and, once again, heartwarming.

My goal for this book is to provide a project for every room and every space, a project that can be set in a modern or traditional environment, for a tiny baby or that tiny baby's grandmother. Whether it be a clean white room with a hint of something handmade or an eclectic country home filled with memories, each project is sure to find its own place—a place in your home as well as a place in your heart.

–Megan

Getting Started

First and foremost, don't hurry. Embroidery takes time to perfect and learn. You don't have to finish in one sitting. Keep your project in a special place and pull it out when you need a little craft time.

Lefties, listen up! The stitching how-to illustrations shown are for the right-handed. If you are left-handed, simply work the stitches in the opposite direction.

As your collection of embroidery floss grows, get organized. I use DMC floss bobbins and floss bobbin containers. This keeps each color in its own space without becoming a tangled mess.

Choose quality fabric that will last so that you can keep your hard work for years to come! Linen is a great choice because it's strong and holds its shape well.

Each project lists the embroidery thread colors that are required. I use DMC floss and pearl cottons. Most floss brands offer a conversion chart if you choose another manufacturer. If you do not use DMC, be sure to select threads that are equally colorfast so they don't run in the washer.

If a project calls for satin stitches, it is easiest to do them first. Otherwise it is challenging to fit them neatly between the other stitches.

Use a hoop? Or don't! I don't use an embroidery hoop, simply because they are too restricting for my freebird hands. However, they can be handy. I'd suggest trying with and without.

Work from the center of a design out to keep your fabric from bunching.

Keep the back of your work neat and tidy. Trim long strings and try not to skip around, leaving long stitches on the back. Sometimes the back of your design can show through or cause bunching, so prevent that with tidiness.

I like to iron my embroidery and appliqué projects once they are finished. It makes them look crisp and neat. When doing this, be sure to lay a scrap piece of fabric on top of the stitching, just in case your iron is dirty or too hot. You don't want to chance ruining your hard work! I also like a little steam on my iron.

When embroidering, it is very helpful to have something behind your fabric to stabilize it. You may use a muslin or cotton solid, or a lightweight tearaway stabilizer such as 360 E-Z Stitch by Pellon, which is perforated and designed for machine embroidery (but that doesn't mean we can't use it for hand embroidery).

To use, cut a piece the same size as the fabric you are embroidering on, place it under the fabric, and secure each corner with a safety pin. Once your embroidery is finished, you can tear away the excess. If you do not tear it away, it will melt to your fabric when you iron it. This won't necessarily hurt your project, but it can create air bubbles and also stick to your iron.

Washing instructions for embroidery: Most folks would say hand wash, lay flat to dry and follow with a warm iron. I have never had any trouble with a gentle machine cycle and a low-heat dryer setting, but I'm no cleaning expert. Please use caution and handle your projects with care.

Feel free to experiment. I see people all the time who can't bring themselves to change any color on an embroidery pattern. I say, go wild! We choose the fabric we want, so why not our own floss colors? Don't write off an embroidery pattern because it's not in "your" colors.

Lastly, perfection is not my goal and need not be yours. Hand stitching is just that: handwork, not machine work. Mess-ups happen, and personally I prefer my stitches organic. In some cases I like my work to be obviously organic; I purposely place my knots and ties on the right side of the work and vary the length of my stitches. Imperfections whether done purposely or not add character, and everything needs character!

Terms to know

Floss = Embroidery floss is made up of six strands of cotton which can be easily separated or combined to adjust the thickness.

Pearl cotton = Pearl cotton is a tightly twisted thread of cotton made up of many strands. It is used as one thread, not separated as floss is. Pearl cotton comes in sizes 3 and 5.

Skein = One individual pack of embroidery floss or pearl cotton.

Strand = A skein of floss is made up of six strands. A person may use as little as one strand or as many as all six.

WOF = Width of fabric

Shorthand guide

Here are some symbols you will see throughout the book and what they mean:

- - - - - - - - - -
cutting line

· · · · · · · · · ·
sewing line

cut   hand stitch

trace or transfer

Basic sewing and stitching supplies

Sewing machine (as needed; including a zipper foot) and iron

Assorted threads, floss and pearl cotton

Lightweight tearaway stabilizer, such as 360 E-Z Stitch (see page 6)

Fusible web*, such as sewable HeatnBond or Wonder-Under (see page 12)

Fusible fleece* (to add thickness to a project, when desired)

Scissors (never use your sewing scissors for paper; they get yucky)

Seam ripper (we all mess up at times)

Tape measure and grid ruler

Rotary cutter and cutting mat

Washable or iron-off fabric pen

Straight pins and safety pins

Hand sewing needles (small appliqué needle and size 22 chenille needle**)

Light source and tracing or transferring supplies (see page 12)

Embroidery hoop, if desired

*Be sure to follow the manufacturer's instructions when using any fusible product. ** Chenille needles are similar to tapestry needles but have sharper points, so handle with care.*

Basic Stitches and Techniques

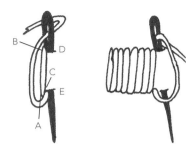

Satin stitch

Work from left to right. Bring the needle up at A, down at B, up at C, down at D and up at E. Repeat as required. Stitches should be close together with no fabric showing between them.

Running stitch

Work from left to right. Bring the thread up at A, down at B, up at C and down at D, and continue. The spaces between the stitches can be the same length as the stitches or shorter for a different look.

Whipped running stitch

Begin with a running stitch. Once the running stitch is complete, begin working it with a whipped stitch. Begin at A and pass the needle under each stitch from top to bottom without piercing the fabric. Pass the needle through the back at the center top of the last stitch.

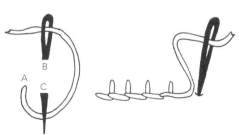

Blanket stitch

Working from left to right, the lower twisted edge forms at the lower line. Bring the needle up at A, down at B and up at C, with the thread looped under the needle. Pull through. Tighten the stitches equally as you go for a neat twisted edge. Fasten down the last loop by taking a small stitch along the lower line.

Backstitch

Work from right to left. Bring the needle up at A, down at B, up at C, then back down at A. Continue stitching. For curved lines and shapes, use small stitches.

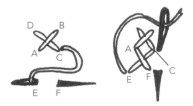

Marking cross stitch

Work from top to bottom. Bring the needle up at A, down at B, up at C, down at D, up at B and down at A. Now, take the needle up at C, down at E and up at F. Next, go down at A, up at E and down at C. Bring the needle up again at F to begin the next repeat.

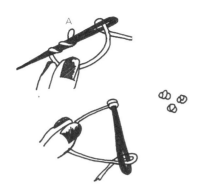

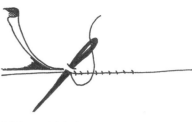

French knot

Bring the needle up at A. Holding the thread taut with your left thumb and index finger, wind the thread tightly around the needle tip twice. Still holding the thread, insert the needle very close to point A and pull through to the back of the work, so the twists lay neatly on the fabric surface. Repeat if required.

Lazy daisy stitch

You may work in any direction. Bring the needle up at A and insert it at the same place, leaving a loop of thread on the surface. Then bring the needle up at B, inside the loop, and down at C, outside the loop, making a tiny stitch to hold the loop in place. Repeat six times to form the daisy shape.

Slip stitch

Use to close openings without the thread showing. Fold each side of the opening fabric under as if for a hem. Start inside of the fold. Hide your knot in the fold. Right next to where you started, on the other side, pick up with your needle just a few threads in the fabric. Then go back down into the fold of the hem. Only grab the fabric that is folded inside. The needle will follow that fold, so the thread stays hidden as you make your seam. Repeat until the opening is closed.

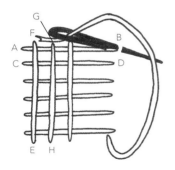

Couched filling stitch

First work long horizontal stitches across the shape, working from top to bottom: Bring the thread up at A, down at B, up at C and down at D. Repeat to the lower edge. Now make long vertical stitches, working from left to right: bring the needle up at E, down at F, up at G and down at H. Repeat to fill the shape. Then work two small diagonal tying stitches across each intersection.

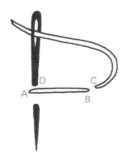

Single buttonhole bar stitch

Bring the needle up at A, down at B, up a tiny distance away at C and down at D. Bring the needle out again just below A to begin the buttonhole stitch. To work the buttonhole you will use the same stitch as in a blanket stitch, but place the stitches very close together, with no fabric showing between them. Work from left to right over the two long stitches without piercing the fabric. (It helps to mark out your teardrop shape before stitching.) Once finished, cut the fabric from the middle of the buttonhole.

Twilling

Twilling, also known as the Palestrina stitch, is a three-step knot repeated consecutively and works best for borders and outlining. If you are not familiar with twilling, practice on a fabric scrap to get a good feel for it.

This stitch is always worked toward you and hoopless. You will be using Size 5 pearl cotton thread, which you will cut into 25 pieces as follows. Each piece covers approximately 5½" (14cm).

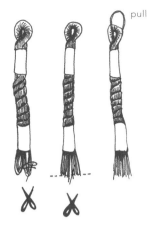

Unrolling and cutting a pearl cotton skein

One end of a skein will have two loops, one of which has a little tie around it. First, cut the tie off. Next, cut through the bottom of both loops. Now you can pull a strand from the opposite end.

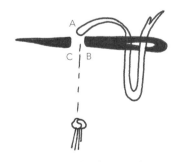

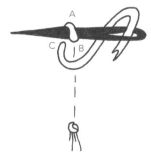

1. With a knot tied at the end of your pearl cotton, place it into your fabric with the knot showing on the right side. Pull it up (point A) about 1½" (3.8cm) from the knot.

Begin working from point A. Move down ⅛" (3mm) to go in at B and come up at C.

2. Work the needle under thread A-B but stay on top of the fabric, only going under your thread.

3. Pull snug, exposing the bottom of stitch A-B. After a few knots, you will get a feel for the correct tension.

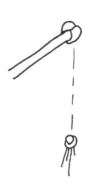

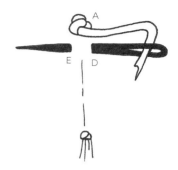

4. Slide the needle under the bottom leg of the A-B stitch. Stay on top of the fabric and thread, working only around the A-B stitch. Do not catch the previous stitch. You may need to flip up the previous stitch in order to not catch it.

5. Pull snug again. This makes two wraps and one completed stitch.

6. Place needle in at D and out at E. Wrap twice like before (steps 2–5), repeating the small stitches and the two wraps as you work your way down the design.

7. This makes two complete stitches. Take your time and use your fingers to hold the fabric and create tension (thumb and index finger on top, and your other three fingers underneath as you stitch). Once you have worked down to the knot, you will cut it off and continue on.

The second illustration shows you what the back of your work will look like for the first 1 " (2.5cm) or so. The stitches need to cover the thread tail since there is no knot to keep the thread from coming loose.

8. To finish a strand of pearl cotton, slide the needle under five or six stitches and pull through. Trim off the extra and do not tie any knots on the back.

To begin a new strand, start it in the same manner as the first strand, fitting your first stitch snug against your last stitch.

Tracing

To trace an embroidery design onto your fabric, you will need a light source (a light box or lit window) and a washable or iron-off fabric pen or pencil. I use Pilot FriXion pens because their heat-activated marks disappear with a quick iron. I also like the Sewline Fabric Pencil, which washes away with water. Begin by placing your design template on your light source and your fabric over the template. Then trace the design onto the fabric.

Transferring

Transferring a design is useful for fabrics too thick or textured for tracing. The first way you can transfer is with transfer paper, which works like a carbon copy. Lay your design on top of the paper, place it on your fabric and trace over it. I like Saral brand because it washes out with water and the paper can be reused.

Another way to transfer is with a transfer pen or pencil. You trace over the design, place it right side down onto the fabric, and iron, leaving behind your tracing marks. With this method, your design needs to be backwards at the start so that the forward version will show on the fabric.

I prefer General's transfer pencils because their marks wash away with water and they are reasonably priced. Most transfer pens are permanent, which leaves no room for error. If your stitches don't cover the marks, your project won't look its best.

Appliqué

Appliqué consists of cutting a shape or design from one fabric and applying it on top of another fabric. The process is made easier by applying fusible web, an iron-on adhesive. I use sewable HeatnBond or Wonder-Under, but many varieties are available.

Start by drawing or tracing your design (backwards) onto the paper side of your fusible web. Next, iron the opposite side of the fusible web to the wrong side of your appliqué fabric. Cut out the shapes, peel off the paper backing and iron them to the right side of your background fabric. Finish by stitching around the edges. Always follow the manufacturer's instructions when using any fusible product.

Raw-edge and needle-turn appliqué

These methods of appliqué do not use fusible web. For raw-edge appliqué, simply stitch just inside the edge of each shape, leaving it "raw." For needle-turn appliqué, cut out your shapes with a ¼" (6mm) seam allowance and use a slip stitch to attach the pieces. Turn the edges under as you sew.

Quilting

Quilting involves sandwiching one layer of batting between two layers of fabric, then sewing all three layers together, giving your quilted item thickness, durability and a decorative surface.

Layer your quilt top, batting and backing fabric together so the wrong sides of each fabric face the batting. Your batting and backing should be 3"–6" (7.6cm to 15.2cm) bigger than your top. You may quilt by hand, on your home machine or on a professional quilting machine.

If quilting at home, baste your quilt (placing safety pins throughout) to hold the layers in place. A basting spray can also be helpful.

Remember to choose a quilting pattern and thread that complements your quilt. Once finished, trim the excess batting and backing, and bind.

If you opt to quilt without backing fabric when the backing won't show, as I have done in some of the projects, be sure to select a sturdy, tightly woven batting.

Binding

Follow these instructions to neatly bind the edges of a quilt. Begin by cutting your binding strips 2½" (6.4cm) wide. Each quilt pattern will note how many strips are required.

1. Join all of your strips together using a 45-degree diagonal seam (right sides together). Cut the excess fabric from each diagonal meeting.

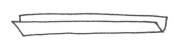

2. Fold the binding in half lengthwise (wrong sides together) and press.

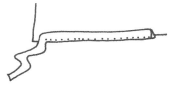

3. Place the binding along one edge of your quilt top, matching the raw edges of the binding with the raw edge of the quilt. Starting a few inches (centimeters) both from the beginning of your binding strip and into one side of your quilt, use a ⅜" (10mm) seam to sew along the edge. Stop and backstitch ¼" (6mm) from the corner.

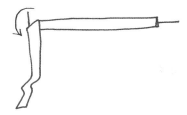

4. Remove from your machine and fold the binding back at a 90-degree angle.

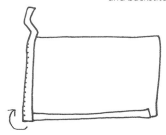

5. Fold the binding forward again along the second edge. Continue to sew the second side starting ¼" (6mm) away from the corner, backstitching at the beginning. Continue using this method for the remaining sides. Cut the end of your binding a couple of inches (centimeters) longer than you will need. Fold the end in at a 90-degree angle and tuck the opposite end of the binding into it. Continue sewing until you have returned to your starting point.

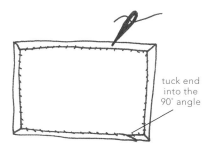

tuck end into the 90° angle

6. Fold the binding toward the back of the quilt, making sure it covers the stitched seam. Use one width of thread to slip stitch the binding down to the back of the quilt. Each corner will be tucked in.

1

Living It Up and Dining In

STATIC dish towel

STACKED framed art

WREATH OF ROSES pillow

THE STUMP stool

CORNER CRESCENT tablecloth

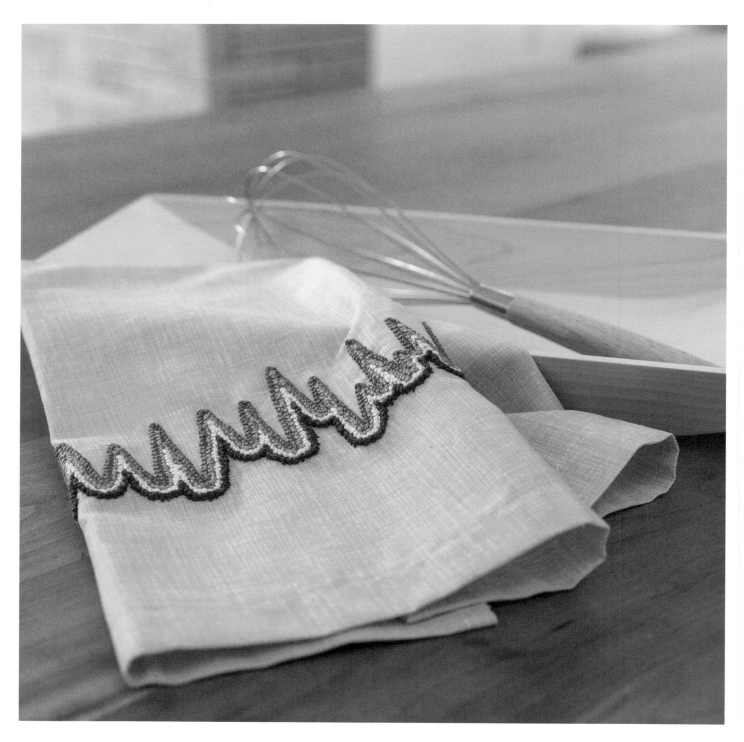

Static dish towel

- -

Dish towels are an essential part of any kitchen. They look great on a stove handle, towel holder or neatly folded. I don't know about you, but my kitchen feels super-naked without a pretty tea towel. Let this electric tea towel add personality to your home with its great color and texture!

FINISHED SIZE

15½" × 26" (39.4cm × 66cm)

FABRIC

½ yard (0.5m) per towel (more may be needed if using a directional print)

TECHNIQUES USED

Tracing (page 12)

Twilling (page 10)

SUPPLIES

Template (page 19)

Washable or iron-off fabric pen and light source

Lightweight tear-away stabilizer: 5" × 16" (12.7cm × 40.6cm)

4 colors of size 5 pearl cotton (shown: DMC no. 225,no. 351, no. 938, no. 4130/variegated)

Size 22 chenille needle

Cutting

From the fabric, cut (1) 17½" × 30" (44.5cm × 76.2cm).

Sewing

NOTE: All seams are ¼" (6mm).

1. Fold each 30" (76.2cm) side over ½" (13mm) and press. Fold over an additional ½" (13mm) and press again. Sew down each side, backstitching at the beginning and end.

2. Repeat the same process for the 17½" (44.5cm) sides, but replace the ½" (13mm) folds with 1" (25mm) folds (Figure 1).

Twilling

1. Before you begin tracing, draw a horizontal line across your sewn towel, placing the line 4" (10.2cm) up from the bottom.

2. Using the template provided, line up the bottom of the design with your horizontal line and trace the design onto your dish towel. The template is designed to repeat; line up one side of the template with the edge of your towel, trace and repeat (Figure 2). Then place your stabilizer under

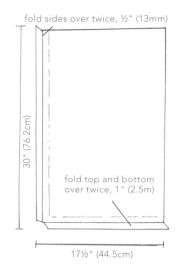

fold sides over twice, ½" (13mm)

30" (76.2cm)

fold top and bottom over twice, 1" (2.5m)

17½" (44.5cm)

Figure 1

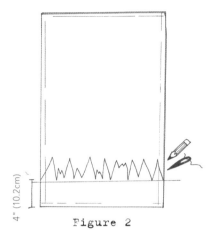

4" (10.2cm)

Figure 2

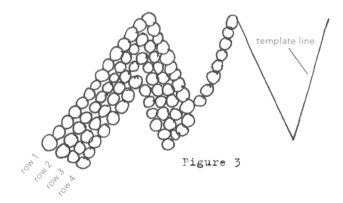

template line

row 1 row 2 row 3 row 4

Figure 3

the design, and safety pin each corner.

3. The template you have traced is the guide for the first color in the design. There are no tracing lines for the next three rows of twilling. Simply follow the guide of the first line, making sure to fit each row snugly together (Figure 3) until you've completed the design.

DMC pearl cotton colors:

no. 4130　no. 351　no. 225　no. 938

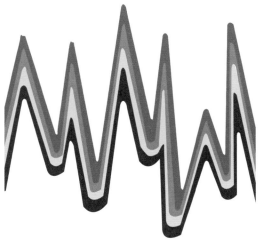

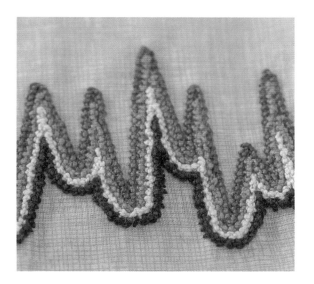

Color/stitching guide
All rows are made with twilling and sit tightly together.

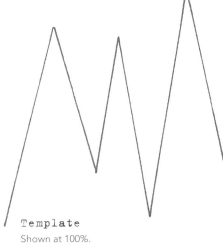

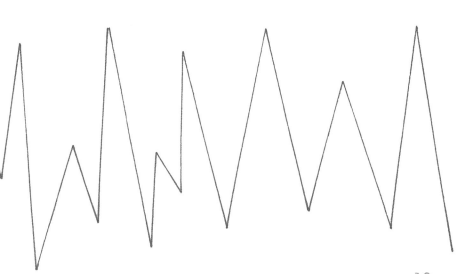

Template
Shown at 100%.

Stacked framed art

I am constantly intrigued and mesmerized by the design of vintage electronics, especially their silhouettes. This embroidery shows off just that, timeless yet modern radios stacked to perfection. I can see this art in almost every room of my home, from being propped on a buffet full of whimsical treasures to hanging in a sleek white office. Feel free to showcase your favorite color; working with a color you love makes for extra-happy stitching!

FINISHED EMBROIDERY

10½" × 6" (26.7cm × 15.2cm)

FABRIC

¾ yard (0.7m) white linen

TECHNIQUES USED

Tracing (page 12)

Backstitch (page 8)

Satin stitch (page 8)

SUPPLIES

Template (page 23)

Washable or iron-off fabric pen and light source

Lightweight tear-away stabilizer: 9" × 12" (22.9cm × 30.5cm)

3 skeins of 1 color of embroidery floss
(shown: DMC no. 349)

Size 22 chenille needle

Frame: 16" × 20" (40.6cm × 50.8cm)

White cardboard, cut to size of inside edge of frame

Adhesive tape

Cutting

From the white linen, cut (1) 22" × 26" (55.9cm × 66cm).

DMC floss color:

no. 349

Embroidery

1. Begin by tracing the template onto the center of your white linen.

2. Once traced, place the linen right side up, directly on top of your stabilizer. Center it under your design, then place a safety pin in each corner to secure the stabilizer.

all solid red areas: satin stitch (3 strands)

all single lines: backstitch (3 strands)

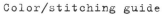

Color/stitching guide

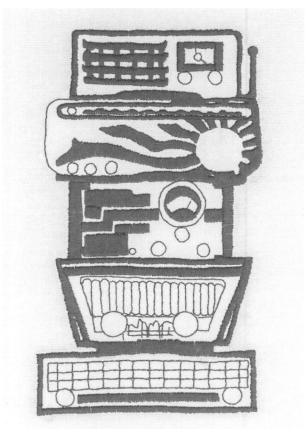

3. Now you can stitch! Refer to the color/stitching guide.

4. Once finished, tear the stabilizer off from around the design and give your art a good pressing.

NOTE: Tear-away stabilizer will stick to your iron if it comes directly in contact with it. To iron your embroidery, place a scrap piece of fabric on top of the design and press gently.

Framing

All done! Now you can frame your super-sleek art. When framing fabric, I like to cut a piece of white cardboard to the size of the inside edge of the frame, center the design and fold the sides around the edges of the cardboard. Secure it tautly in place with adhesive tape.

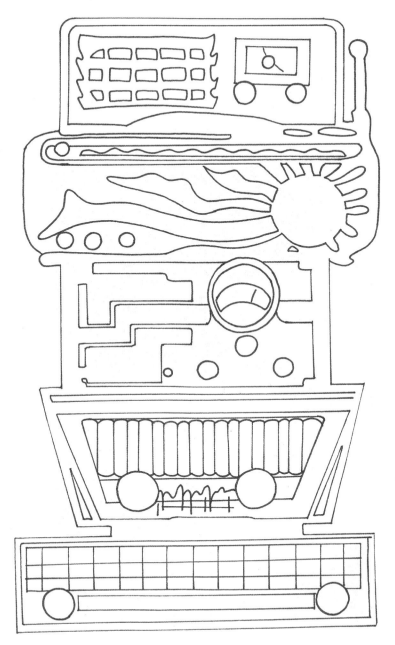

Template
Enlarge at 160%.

Wreath of Roses pillow

This embroidery design has a great vibe that can work in so many spaces. Because roses are timeless, the look of your pillow is really determined by your fabric choices. You can make it to fit any room or style.

FINISHED SIZE

18" (45.7cm) square

FABRIC

Front main: 1 fat quarter

Front accent: 1 fat eighth

Linen (for embroidery): 14" (35.6cm) square

Back: ½ yard (0.5m)

Note: Fabric requirements may need to be increased if your fabric is directional. A fat quarter is measured by folding a yard of fabric in fourths so each piece is approximately 18" × 22" (45.7cm × 55.9cm).

TECHNIQUES USED

Tracing (page 12) or Transferring (page 12)

Satin stitch (page 8)

Quilting (page 12)

Raw-edge appliqué (page 12)

SUPPLIES

Template (page 29)

Tracing or transferring tools

Lightweight tear-away stabilizer: 14" (35.6cm) square

5 colors of embroidery floss (shown: DMC no. 349, no. 351, no. 780, no. 816, no. 3779)

Size 22 chenille needle

Batting (tightly woven): 1 yard (0.9m)

18" (45.7cm) square pillow form

DMC floss colors:

no. 816   no. 349   no. 351   no. 3779   no. 780

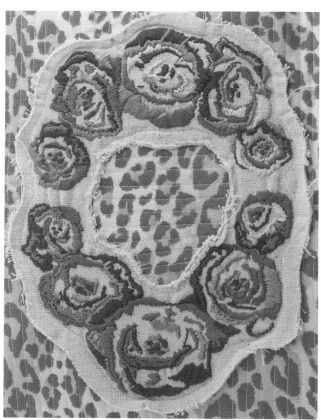

Color/stitching guide

All stitches are satin stitch (3 strands).

Cutting

From the front main fabric, cut:
(1) 14" × 19" (35.6cm × 48.3cm)

From the front accent fabric, cut:
(1) 5½" × 19" (14cm × 48.3cm)

From the back fabric, cut:
(1) 15" × 19" (38.1cm × 48.3cm)
(1) 11" × 19" (27.9cm × 48.3cm)

Embroidery

1. Using your piece of linen and stabilizer, trace or transfer your embroidery design using the provided template on page 29.

NOTE: If you are transferring, remember to place your design backwards.

2. Follow the color/stitching guide to complete the satin stitch embroidery.

Sewing

NOTE: Remember to sew right sides together and to press as you sew. Seams are ¼" (6mm) unless otherwise noted.

1. Begin by piecing your two front pieces together as shown in Figure 1. This is your top piece.

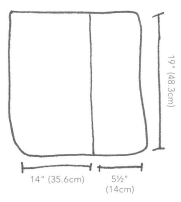

14" (35.6cm)   5½" (14cm)

19" (48.3cm)

Figure 1

quilting   batting

Figure 2

2. Next, layer the top as well as the two back pieces with the batting and quilt (Figure 2).

3. Once your pieces are quilted, trim down the top piece to 18½" × 18½" (47cm × 47cm). Trim each back piece down as well. The big piece will be trimmed to 14" × 18½" (35.6cm × 47cm) and the smaller of the two to 10" × 18½" (25.4cm × 47cm).

4. Now, take out your embroidery and cut out the shape, leaving a ½" (13mm) seam allowance.

5. Center the design onto the main fabric of your quilted pillow top. Using raw-edge appliqué, attach it to the pillow, using a ¼" (6mm) seam (Figure 3).

6. On each back piece, fold one 18½" (47cm) side over ½" (13mm) toward the wrong side twice and sew (Figure 4).

7. With wrong sides together, place the biggest back piece onto the top, lining up the outside 18½" (47cm) raw edges, and sew the three sides. Repeat with the smaller back piece, backstitching at each end (Figure 5).

8. Turn your pillow inside out and insert your pillow form.

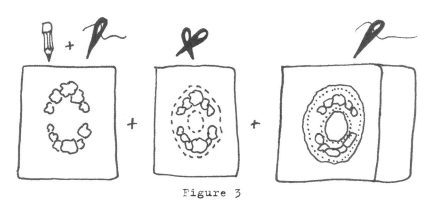

Figure 3

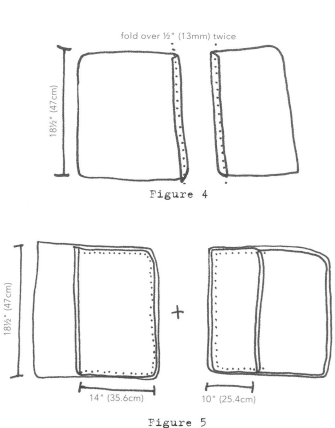

fold over ½" (13mm) twice

18½" (47cm)

Figure 4

18½" (47cm)

14" (35.6cm)

10" (25.4cm)

Figure 5

Template
Enlarge at 125%.

The Stump stool

- -

What's the first thing I do when I sit down to hand stitch? Put my feet up, of course! Literally, there's an ottoman at every chair in my home. This stool has a raw simplicity about it that calls to me. It's the perfect size for a pair of feet or even a bottom. Don't let its light and airy look fool you; it's very sturdy.

FINISHED SIZE

18" × 18" × 18" (45.7cm × 45.7cm × 45.7cm)

FABRIC

Linen: 1⅞ yards (1.7m)

Appliqué fabric: 6" × 20" (15.2cm × 50.8cm), or 1 fat eighth

TECHNIQUES USED

Quilting (page 12)

Appliqué (page 12)

Blanket stitch (page 8)

Marking cross stitch (page 8)

SUPPLIES

Batting (tightly woven): 1⅞ yards (1.7m)

Washable or iron-off fabric pen

Round plate

Fusible web: 6" × 20" (15.2cm × 50.8cm)

3 colors of embroidery floss: 1 for side stitching and 2 for appliqué (shown: DMC no. 600, no. 728, no. 964)

Size 22 chenille needle

Beanbag filling: 100 liters/26.4 gallons

Note: I like Bean Bag Factory's Bag of Beans, available online and in many stores.

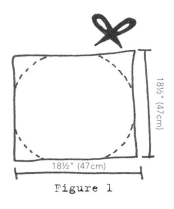

Figure 1

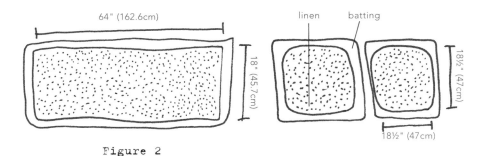

Figure 2

Cutting

From the linen, cut:
(1) 18" × 64" (45.7cm × 162.6cm)
(2) 18½" × 18½" (47cm × 47cm)

From the appliqué fabric, cut:
(1) 4" × 18" (10.2cm × 45.7cm). Iron on fusible web, then cut into (4) 1" × 18" (2.5cm × 45.7cm) strips.

From the batting, cut:
(1) 22" × 66" (55.9cm × 167.6cm)
(2) 20" × 20" (50.8cm × 50.8cm)

Use a round plate to help you round the corners on the two square pieces of linen (the stool top and bottom). Simply place the plate on each corner, trace the line with a washable or iron-off fabric pen, and cut off the corners (Figure 1). This will leave you with a "squoval" shape. Make sure to use the first as a template for the second so they are the same shape.

Quilting

Begin by layering the side, top and bottom pieces with batting and quilting them (Figure 2). These pieces are easy to quilt on your own machine, but be sure to use a dense quilting pattern. The quilting is what helps make the stool sturdy.

Once your quilting is finished, trim the excess batting.

Appliqué

1. Peel off the paper backing from your 1" × 18" (2.5cm × 45.7cm) strips and iron the strips in an "X" on the top and bottom pieces. Once your pieces are in place, blanket stitch (6 strands) around the edges of each "X" (Figure 3).

NOTE: I used three floss colors, one for each appliquéd "X" and one for the side closure. I used big stitches and didn't hide my knots. It adds a fun flair to the rugged look of the stump stool.

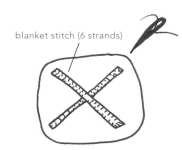

Figure 3

Sewing

1. Once your hand stitching is done, begin constructing your stool. Before you start sewing, place the top and bottom pieces wrong sides together and mark the middle of one side on each piece with a straight pin.

2. Pin your side piece around your top piece, placing wrong sides together. You'll be starting at the point where you placed the straight pin.

3. Using a ⅜" (10mm) seam, sew the top to the side. Once you get back to your pinned starting point, continue sewing until each end meets. Do not overlap your sewing; just stop where they meet. The side will be slightly longer, but do not trim it yet.

4. Beginning at the straight pin on your bottom piece, attach it in the same manner as you attached the top in the previous step (Figure 4).

5. Trim the excess side so that the two ends meet together but do not overlap (Figure 5).

6. At each of the cube's four corners, pinch a seam down the side and pin. Starting ½" (13mm)

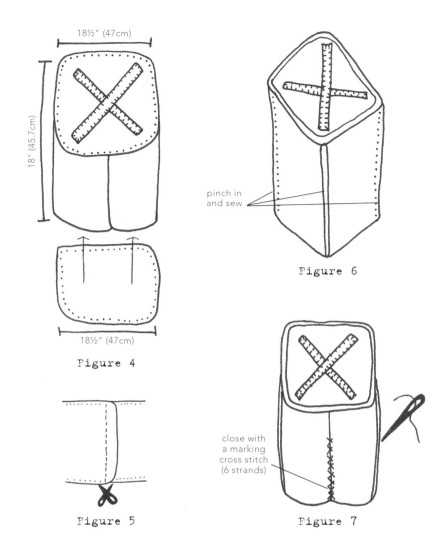

18½" (47cm)

18" (45.7cm)

18½" (47cm)

Figure 4

Figure 5

pinch in and sew

Figure 6

close with a marking cross stitch (6 strands)

Figure 7

from the top, sew a ⅜" (10mm) seam down the side, stopping ½" (13mm) from the bottom (Figure 6). Don't forget to backstitch at the beginning and end.

7. Using a marking cross stitch (6 strands), close the side opening halfway. Fill your stool with the beanbag filling, but do not overfill. Once it is stuffed, close the rest of the opening (Figure 7).

Corner Crescent tablecloth

A handmade tablecloth can add a comfortable feel to any room. Linens can become heirlooms as easily as quilts. At my house, table décor is reserved for special occasions. Whether it's a beautiful birthday, a romantic dinner or a grand holiday party, you can guarantee that I will pull out my best tablecloths. This one is simple in design but can be made grand with your fabric choice. I added a little dip dye to mine!

FINISHED SIZE

51" (129.5cm) square

FABRIC

54" (137.2cm) wide fabric (linen shown):
1½ yards (1.4m)

TECHNIQUES USED

Tracing (page 12) or Transferring (page 12)

Satin stitch (page 8)

SUPPLIES

1 package of dip dye

1 rubber band

Template (page 37)

Tracing or transferring tools

Lightweight tear-away stabilizer: 12" × 12"
(30.5cm × 30.5cm)

1 color of embroidery floss (shown: DMC no. 349)

Size 22 chenille needle

Cutting

From your linen or other chosen fabric, cut:
(1) 52" × 52" (132.1cm × 132.1cm)

Dyeing

I chose to apply a colorful dip dye to the fabric first. To do this, gather and wrap a rubber band around one side of your fabric.

Following the manufacturer's instructions, place the gathered fabric into the dye and leave for the recommended time. Once finished, wash and dry your fabric before continuing.

Sewing

Fold each side of your fabric over ½" (13mm) twice. Press and finish with a ⅜" (10mm) seam (Figure 1).

Embroidery

1. Using the template provided, trace or transfer your design to one corner of your tablecloth (Figure 2).

2. Place the stabilizer directly behind your embroidery design, and safety pin each corner.

3. Embroider your design, referring to the color/stitching guide. Once finished, tear away the stabilizer.

DMC floss color: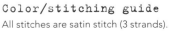

no. 349

Color/stitching guide
All stitches are satin stitch (3 strands).

fold over ½" (13mm) twice

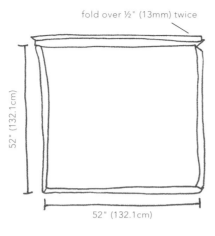

52" (132.1cm)

52" (132.1cm)

Figure 1

Figure 2

Template
Enlarge at 135%.

2

Treat Me Sweet and Put Me to Bed

URBAN DIAMONDS master quilt

MORNING ROSES robe

MR. DEER and DEAREST DEER travel cases

SEED STITCHED shams

SCRIBBLES laundry tote

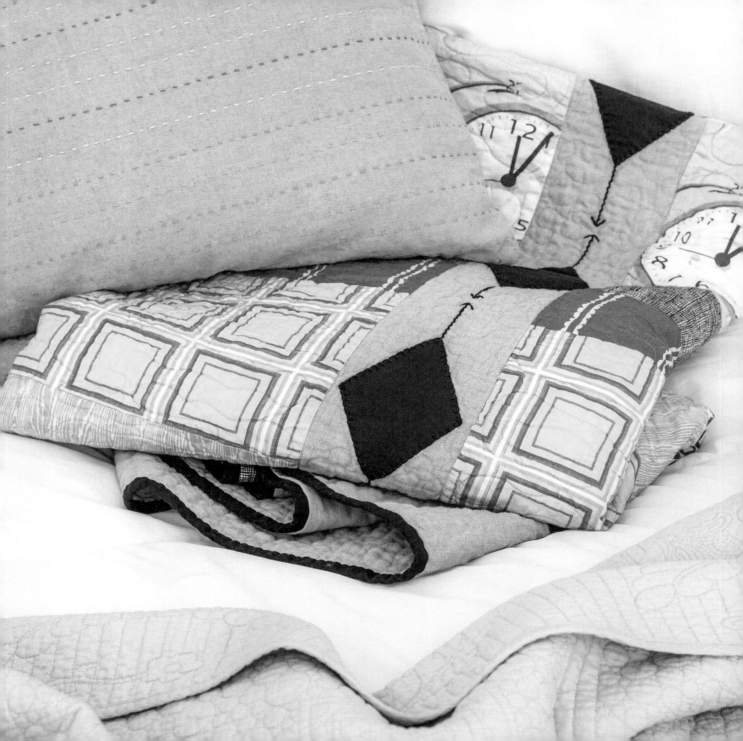

Urban Diamonds master quilt

You know that amazing quilt you snuggle with every night? What? You don't have one? Well, this is it! This quilt is an eclectic blend of modern, urban and vintage sure to suit any bedroom. The soft cotton and linen fabrics will keep you cool on a summer night and warm on those frosty ones.

FINISHED SIZE

Full, 79" × 86" (200.7cm × 218.4cm)

FABRIC

Main focal print (quilt center): 1⅛ yards (1m)

Secondary focal print: 1⅛ yards (1m)

5 accent prints: ⅝ yard (0.6m) of each

Solid for Border 1 and appliqué: 1¼ yards (1.1m)

Linen for Border 2 and sashing: 1⅔ yards (1.5m) of 54" (137.2cm) linen, or 2⅜ yards (2.2m) of 45" (114.3cm) linen

Backing: 91" × 98" (231.1cm × 248.9cm)

Binding: ¾ yard (.7m)

← Pieced by Megan Frock
Quilted by Jessica Defibaugh

TECHNIQUES USED

Tracing (page 12)

Appliqué (page 12)

Blanket stitch (page 8)

Whipped running stitch (page 8)

Quilting (page 12) and Binding (page 13)

SUPPLIES

Templates (page 44)

Tracing or transferring tools

Washable or iron-off fabric pen and light source

Fusible web: ⅔ yard (.6m)

3 skeins of 1 color of embroidery floss (black shown)

Size 22 chenille needle

Batting: 91" × 98" (231.1cm × 248.9cm)

Cutting

From your main focal print, cut (2) 18" × WOF (45.7cm × WOF).

From your secondary focal print, cut (4) 9" × WOF (22.9cm × WOF).

From each of your 5 accent prints, cut (4) 4½ × WOF (11.4cm × WOF).

For the sashing, from your linen fabric cut 4 strips, each 5" × WOF (12.7cm × WOF). NOTE: If your fabric is 45" (114.3cm) wide instead of a 54" (137.2) linen, you will need 5 strips instead of 4.

For Border 1, from your solid fabric cut 7 strips, each 3" × WOF (7.6cm × WOF).

For Border 2, from your linen fabric cut 6 strips, each 6" × WOF (15.2cm × WOF). NOTE: If your fabric is 45" (114.3cm) instead of a 54" (137.2cm) linen, you will need 8 strips instead of 6.

For the binding, cut 8 strips, each 2½" × WOF (6.4cm × WOF).

Sewing

NOTE: All seams are ¼" (6mm). Make sure you sew your fabric right sides together and press your seams open as you go.

1. Begin by laying out the cuts from your main focal print, secondary focal print and accent prints. (The accent prints will be called accents 1–5.) You can play with their placement to figure out where they look best. Once your pieces are laid out and in order, you can sew the strips together (Figure 1). To do this, place two strips right sides together and repeat until all strips are sewn.

Repeat this process for a second panel.

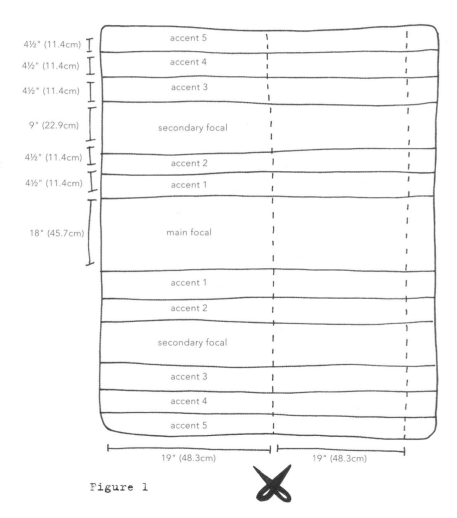

Figure 1

2. After you have two complete panels, you will cut the first panel into three strips. Two of the strips will be 19" (48.3cm) wide and the other will be a small leftover strip about 5" (12.7cm) wide (Figure 1). From the second panel, you will only need to cut one 19" (48.3cm) strip.

NOTE: The leftover from Panel 2 works great for a pieced backing.

3. Set your three main panel strips aside and sew your sashing together. Simply sew all of the sashing strips together end to end to form one long strip. Once you have finished sewing, find the center and cut the strip in half to form two shorter strips.

4. Now, cut your main panels and sashing strips to size. To do this, measure your three main panels and write down the length of the shortest one. Even if it is an odd number, use it! Trim your three panels and your two sashing strips to this same size.

Appliqué

1. Iron your fusible web to the back of your remaining solid fabric. Using the diamond template provided, trace and cut 14 diamonds.

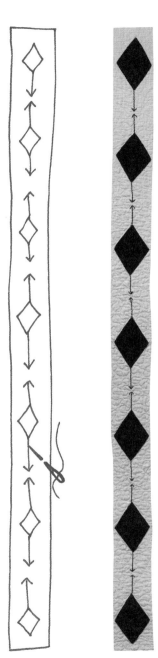

Figure 2

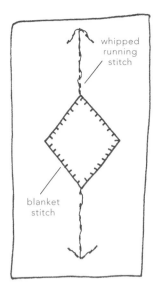

Figure 3

2. Find the center of one of your sashing strips. Place one of the diamond pieces directly in the center, peel off the paper backing and iron it on. From here you will position 3 diamonds on either side, 6" (15.2cm) apart from each other as well as from the center diamond. Between each diamond, trace the double-arrow template with a washable or iron-off fabric pen (Figure 2).

Repeat this step for your second sashing strip.

3. Blanket stitch around each diamond, and do a whipped running stitch for the arrows (Figure 3). All stitches will use 6 strands of floss.

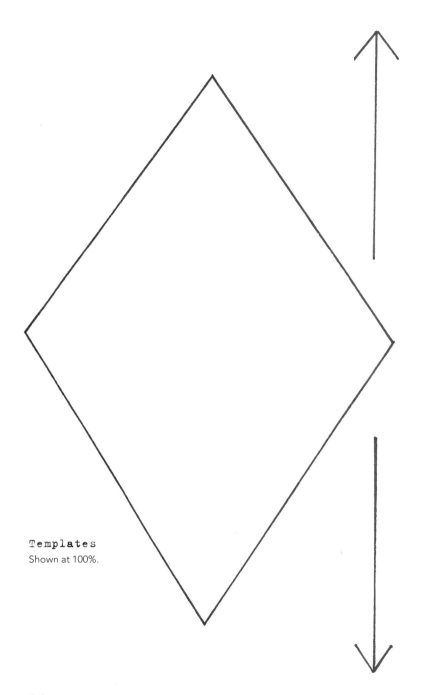

Templates
Shown at 100%.

Back to sewing

1. Once your handwork is done, you can finish piecing. Begin by laying out your three main panels and your two appliquéd sashing strips (Figure 4). Once laid out, sew each piece to the next with right sides together in ¼" (6mm) seams. Press as you sew.

2. Before you begin the borders, give your quilt a good pressing. Then sew all of your Border 1 strips together. Once they are sewn and seams are pressed open, measure the width of your quilt at the horizontal center. Next, take a couple more measurements away from the center but not at the edge. Average these measurements together, and that is the length you will need to cut for your top and bottom borders. Use the exact number you came up with, because the borders must match your quilt. Sew on the top and bottom borders. Repeat this measurement and cutting process on the vertical for the side borders and sew them on as well (Figure 5).

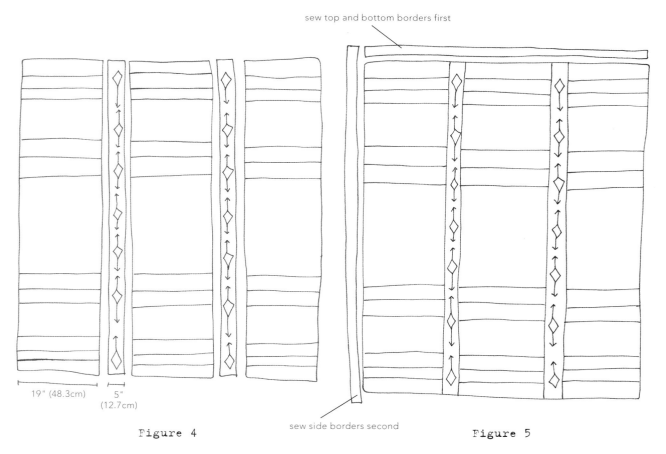

sew top and bottom borders first

sew side borders second

19" (48.3cm)   5" (12.7cm)

Figure 4

Figure 5

3. Press Border 1. Repeat the cutting and sewing process for Border 2 (Figure 6).

Quilting and binding

Once your quilt top is completed, layer and quilt it as desired. Bind your quilt with the 2½" (6.4cm) wide fabric strips.

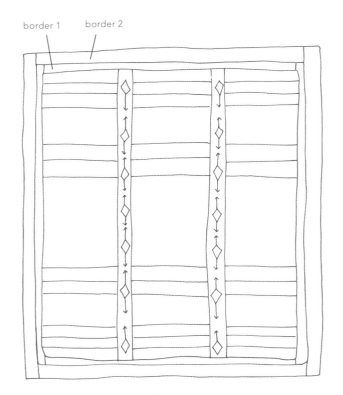

Figure 6

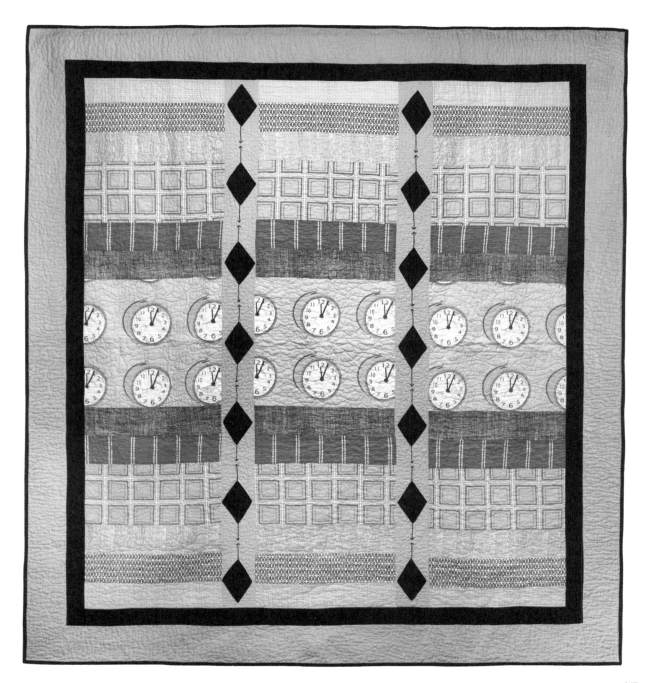

Morning Roses robe

- -

My robe is the first thing I grab when I wake up. I'm sort of a wear-my-pj's-all-day kind of gal, and I wanted something ultra feminine yet presentable. (You know, for when someone unexpectedly knocks on your door and you're still in your pj's.) This robe has quickly become a staple in my wardrobe!

FINISHED EMBROIDERY

9¾" × 7½" (24.8cm × 19.1cm)

FABRIC

1 store-bought, waffle-weave cotton spa robe

White linen: 12" × 15" (30.5cm × 38.1cm)

TECHNIQUES USED

Tracing (page 12) or Transferring (page 12)

Appliqué (page 12)

Satin stitch (page 8)

Backstitch (page 8)

Blanket stitch (page 8)

French knot (page 9)

SUPPLIES

Template (page 51)

Tracing or transferring tools

Fusible web: 12" × 15" (30.5cm × 38.1cm)

Lightweight tear-away stabilizer: 12" × 15" (30.5cm × 38.1cm)

13 colors of embroidery floss (shown: DMC no. 300, no. 307, no. 310, no. 352, no. 892, no. 924, no. 950, no. 964, no. 3023, no. 3072, no. 3802, no. 3851, no. 3852)

Size 22 chenille needle

Round plate

Embroidery

1. Begin by tracing or transferring your design using the template provided onto the center of your white linen (Figure 1).

NOTE: If you are transferring, remember to place your design backwards.

2. Once your design is transferred, place your stabilizer behind your linen and safety pin in place. Now you can begin stitching, following the color/stitching guide. Once your embroidery is complete, tear off the excess stabilizer from the back of your design.

DMC floss colors:

no. 300   no. 950   no. 352   no. 892   no. 3802   no. 310   no. 3023   no. 3072   no. 964   no. 3851   no. 924   no. 3852   no. 307

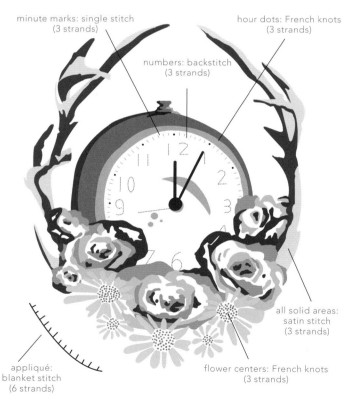

minute marks: single stitch (3 strands)

hour dots: French knots (3 strands)

numbers: backstitch (3 strands)

all solid areas: satin stitch (3 strands)

appliqué: blanket stitch (6 strands)

flower centers: French knots (3 strands)

Color/stitching guide

50

Appliqué

1. Begin by cutting your linen into an oval shape. You can do this by marking with a washable or iron-off fabric pen and a round plate to achieve curved lines, then cut it out. Leave at least 1" (2.5cm) of space around your design.

2. Using your fusible web, iron your embroidered piece to the back of your robe (Figure 2).

NOTE: Center your design between the neckline and belt.

3. Complete your design by using a blanket stitch around the appliqué.

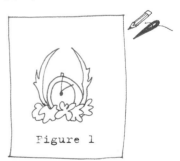

Figure 1

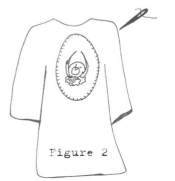

Figure 2

Template
Enlarge at 167%.

Mr. Deer and Dearest Deer travel cases

It seems every time I travel, I end up not having a bag for my bathroom goodies. (OK, I have one, but it's not cute.) Shouldn't style be applied to every part of our lives? This slouchy travel case is so amazing! Fast to whip up, sturdy, convenient and most importantly, stylish — especially a his-and-hers pair of cases.

FINISHED SIZE
13" × 17" (33cm × 43.2cm) each

FABRIC
Outer fabric: ½ yard (0.5m) per bag
Lining fabric: ½ yard (0.5m) per bag

TECHNIQUES USED
Tracing (page 12)
Satin stitch (page 8)
French knot (page 9)
Slip stitch (page 9)

SUPPLIES
Templates (page 55)

Washable or iron-off fabric pen and light source

Fusible fleece: ¾ yard (.7m) per bag

Lightweight tear-away stabilizer: 6" × 11" (15.2cm × 27.9cm) per bag

16" (40.6cm) zipper per bag

¼" (6mm) cording (for zipper pull): 10" (25.4cm) per bag

3 colors of embroidery floss for Mr. Deer case (shown: DMC no. 822, no. 3023, no. 3787); add 4 more colors for Dearest Deer case (shown: DMC no. 165, no. 351, no. 352, no. 833)

Size 22 chenille needle

Small sewing needle

Zipper foot for sewing machine

Cutting

NOTE: The instructions that follow are for making one bag.

From the outer fabric, cut:
(1) 11" × 18" (27.9cm × 45.7cm)
(1) 13" × 18" (33cm × 45.7cm)
(1) 2¼" × 18" (5.7cm × 45.7cm)

From the lining fabric, cut:
(1) 11½" × 17½" (29.2cm × 44.5cm)

(1) 13" × 17½" (33cm × 44.5cm)
(1) 2½" × 17½" (6.4cm × 44.5cm)

From the fusible fleece, cut:
(1) 11" × 18" (27.9cm × 45.7cm)
(1) 13" × 18" (33cm × 45.7cm)
(1) 2¼" × 18" (5.7cm × 45.7cm)

Embroidery

1. Using one of the provided templates, trace your chosen design onto your 11" × 18" (27.9cm × 45.7cm) piece of outer fabric. For placement, refer to Figure 1 (page 56).

2. Before stitching, place stabilizer behind the design and place a safety pin in each corner. Then follow the color/stitching guide as you embroider your design. Once finished, tear off the excess stabilizer.

DMC floss colors

no. 3787   no. 3023   no. 822   no. 165   no. 833   no. 352   no. 351

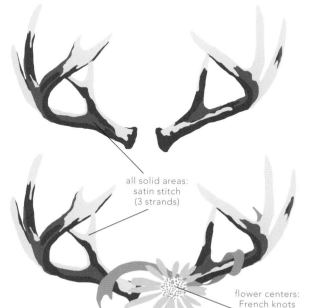

all solid areas:
satin stitch
(3 strands)

flower centers:
French knots
(3 strands)

Color/stitching guide

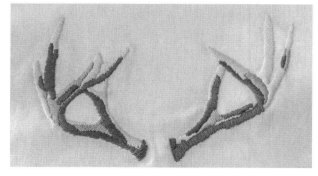

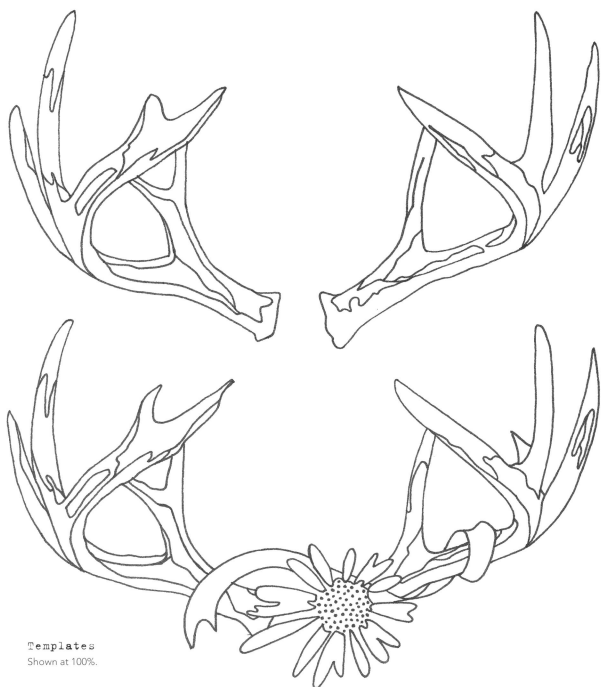

Templates
Shown at 100%.

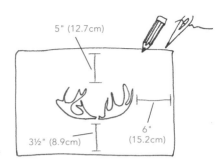

5" (12.7cm)

3½" (8.9cm)

6" (15.2cm)

Figure 1

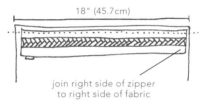

18" (45.7cm)

join right side of zipper
to right side of fabric

Figure 2

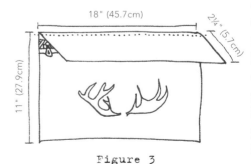

18" (45.7cm)

2¼" (5.7cm)

11" (27.9cm)

Figure 3

Sewing

NOTE: All seams are ¼" (6mm) unless noted, and remember, right sides together.

1. First, iron the fusible fleece pieces to the wrong side of all outer fabric pieces.

2. To construct the outside of the bag, begin by centering your zipper on the top of your embroidered fabric. Place the right side of the zipper on the right side of the fabric (Figure 2). Using a zipper foot on your sewing machine, attach the top strip of the zipper.

3. Using the same method as in step 2, attach the other side of the zipper to the 2¼" × 18" (5.7cm × 45.7cm) outer fabric piece (Figure 3).

4. Next, join the finished zipper side of the bag and the back piece, right sides together. (The back is the 13" × 18" [33cm × 45.7cm] outer fabric piece.) Pin in place and stitch the sides and the bottom (Figure 4). Depending on your particular zipper, you may have to use a bigger seam on the sides so that you can catch the ends. I used a double-sided coat zipper.

5. Time to construct the inside! The large 13" × 17½" (33cm × 44.5cm) piece is your back piece. Lay it down with the right side facing up. On top of it place the two front lining pieces, the small at the top and the bigger at the bottom. Line up the top and bottom edges. The middle will have an overlap, about ½" (13mm) on each side. Pin in place and sew the bottom and sides. On each side where the fabrics meet, stop sewing ½" (13mm) from where the two pieces meet, leaving a 1" (2.5cm) opening (Figure 5).

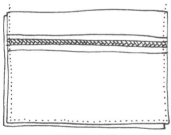

Figure 4

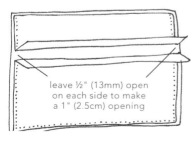

leave ½" (13mm) open
on each side to make
a 1" (2.5cm) opening

Figure 5

6. Turn the outside of the bag right side out and the inside of the bag inside out. Place the inside of the bag over the outside so that the right sides are together. Make sure the zipper sides are together. Sew around the opening of the top (Figure 6) to sew the lining to the bag, but don't sew the bag closed.

7. Once sewn, tuck the lining down into the outside of the bag and finger press the top flat. About ¼" (6mm) of the lining will show on the outside. Sew the top together so that it is closed (Figure 7).

8. Now, turn your bag inside out and pull the lining up to meet each side of the zipper. Fold under and slip stitch into place. You will sew down each side and each end of the zipper (Figure 8).

9. If you wish, you can add a spiffy zipper pull. Simply take your 10" (25.4cm) piece of cording, fold it in half, and sew a zigzag stitch down the center to connect the halves. Leave a ½" (13mm) opening at the fold (Figure 9). Pull the cording through the zipper tab, tuck the raw end through the ½" (13mm) opening, and pull tight (Figure 10).

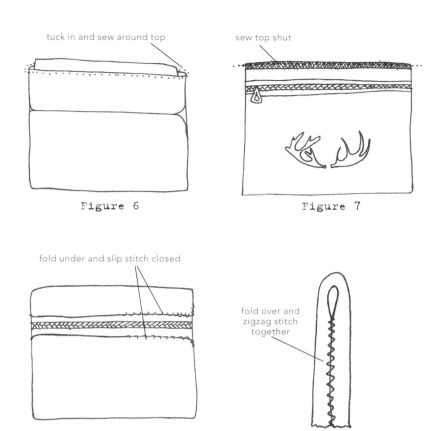

tuck in and sew around top

sew top shut

Figure 6

Figure 7

fold under and slip stitch closed

fold over and zigzag stitch together

Figure 8

Figure 9

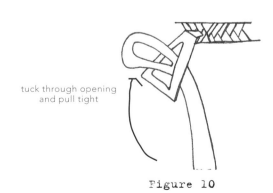

tuck through opening and pull tight

Figure 10

Seed Stitched shams

Have you ever rested your head on linen? Once linen is washed, it makes for the comfiest pillows. I only use linen pillows in my home, and everyone — including kitties — agrees they make for a lovely rest!

FINISHED SIZE

19" × 27" (48.3cm × 68.6cm), for standard-size bed pillow

FABRIC

Linen: 1¼ yards (1.1m) per sham

TECHNIQUE USED

Running stitch (page 8)

SUPPLIES

Washable or iron-off fabric pen

Ruler or straightedge

Batting (tightly woven): 22" × 31" (55.9cm × 78.7cm) per sham

7 colors of embroidery floss (shown: DMC no. 307, no. 597, no. 833, no. 921, no. 955, no. 3023, no. 3846)

Size 22 chenille needle

Standard-size bed pillow

Cutting

NOTE: The instructions that follow are for making one sham.

From the linen, cut:
(1) 20" × 29" (50.8cm × 73.7cm) front
(2) 18" × 20" (45.7cm × 50.8cm) backs

DMC floss colors:

no. 307 no. 955 no. 3846 no. 597 no. 3023 no. 833 no. 921

Color/stitching guide
Each line is a running stitch (6 strands).

Embroidery

1. Begin by drawing stitching guidelines on your 20" × 29" (50.8cm × 73.7cm) piece of linen (Figure 1). Using a ruler, draw 18 horizontal lines, spacing them 1" (2.5cm) apart.

2. Next, center your batting behind your fabric and line up all edges, pinning if desired.

3. Once your lines are drawn and the batting is in place, stitch over the lines, following the color/stitching guide. Trim the batting to size.

Sewing

1. On one back piece, fold one of the 20" (50.8cm) sides over 1" (2.5cm) and press. Fold over one more inch (2.5cm) and press (Figure 2).

2. Use the same technique as in step 1 for the second back piece, but replace the 1" (2.5cm) folds with ½" (13mm) folds. Be sure you are folding a 20" (50.8cm) side and not an 18" (45.7cm) side.

3. Once your two back pieces are folded and pressed, sew a ¼" (6mm) seam on both long edges of the fold (Figure 3).

NOTE: For the remainder of the sewing, use a ¾" (19mm) seam so you can be sure to catch all layers.

4. Time to sew the backs and front together. Begin by laying out your front piece right side up (the side you stitched on) and place one back piece on top, right sides together. The side of the back piece with the flush hem (the smooth, unfolded side) should face the right side of the front piece. This is the "right" side of your back piece. Line up the unhemmed 20" (50.8cm) side of the back piece with one 20" (50.8cm) side of your front piece. Sew these 20" (50.8cm) sides together (Figure 4), backstitching at the beginning and end. Repeat for the second back piece.

5. Next, lay down the back piece with the 1" (2.5cm) hem, right sides together, and align the top and bottom with the front piece. Pin in place and sew the top and bottom. Repeat for the second back piece. The back piece with the 1" (2.5cm) hem should be on the inside, facing the front piece, while the back piece with the ½" (13mm) hem will overlap the first back piece and

face you (Figure 5). Be sure to only sew one back piece at a time to prevent puckering.

6. Once the back and front pieces are sewn, use a zigzag stitch or serge around all sides (Figure 6). This will keep your seams nice and tidy.

7. Turn your sham right side out and press.

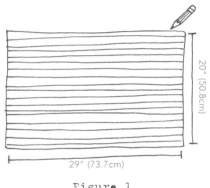

Figure 1

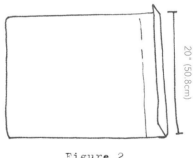

Figure 2

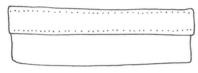

Figure 3

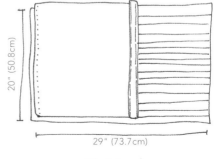

Figure 4

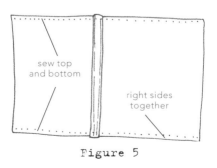

sew top and bottom

right sides together

Figure 5

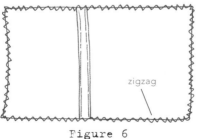

zigzag

Figure 6

Scribbles laundry tote

Laundry is my favorite chore of all time. Just kidding, it is my least favorite! Because of this, I decided a super-cute laundry bag would make the task easier to take. This tote is the perfect size, and the shoulder straps are much more efficient then dragging around a drawstring bag.

FINISHED SIZE

21" × 21" x 8" (53.3cm × 53.3cm ×20.3cm)

FABRIC

Outer fabric (quilter's cotton shown): 1¾ yards (1.6m)

Lining fabric (linen shown): 1¾ yards (1.6m)

TECHNIQUES USED

Tracing (page 12)

Satin stitch (page 8)

Twilling (page 10)

Slip stitch (page 9)

SUPPLIES

Template (page 66)

Tracing tools

Lightweight tear-away stabilizer: 8" × 22" (20.3cm × 55.9cm)

1 color of embroidery floss (shown: DMC no. 720)

1 color of size 5 pearl cotton (shown: DMC no. 818)

Size 22 chenille needle

Small sewing needle

Fusible fleece: 1¾ yards (1.6m)

Cutting

From the outer fabric, cut:
(2) 22" × 26" (55.9cm × 66cm)
(2) 6" × 30" (15.2cm × 76.2cm)
(1) 8½" × 22" (21.6cm × 55.9cm)

From the lining fabric, cut:
(2) 22" × 26" (55.9cm × 66cm)
(2) 6" × 30" (15.2cm × 76.2cm)
(1) 8½" × 22" (21.6cm × 55.9cm)

From the fusible fleece, cut:
(2) 22" × 26" (55.9cm × 66cm)
(2) 6" × 30" (15.2cm × 76.2cm)
(1) 8½" × 22" (21.6cm × 55.9cm)

Embroidery and twilling

1. Using the provided template, trace the design onto one of your 22" × 26" (55.9cm × 66cm) outer fabric pieces. Place the design 6½" (16.5cm) up from the bottom and centered (Figure 1).

2. Before stitching, place your stabilizer behind the design and place a safety pin in each corner. Then embroider and twill the design, following the color/stitching guide.

3. Once you are finished stitching, tear the excess stabilizer off from around your design.

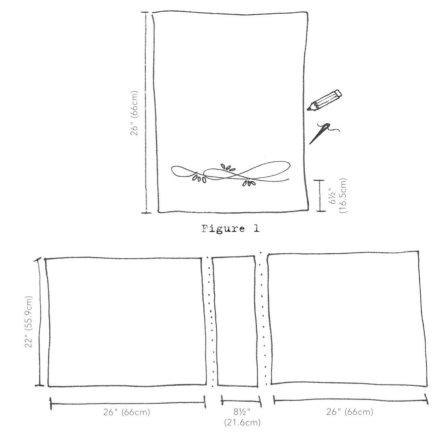

Figure 1

Figure 2

Sewing

NOTE: All seams are ¼" (6mm). Remember to place right sides together and press your seams as you go.

1. Now it's time to construct your bag. Begin by ironing your fusible fleece pieces to the wrong side of your outer fabric pieces.

2. Begin constructing the lining of the bag by sewing the side pieces to the bottom piece. To do this, line up one 22" (55.9cm) side of the front and back pieces to the 22" (55.9cm) sides of the 8½" (21.6cm) bottom piece and stitch, right sides together (Figure 2).

DMC pearl cotton and floss colors:

no. 818   no. 720

satin stitch (3 strands)   twilling (1 strand)

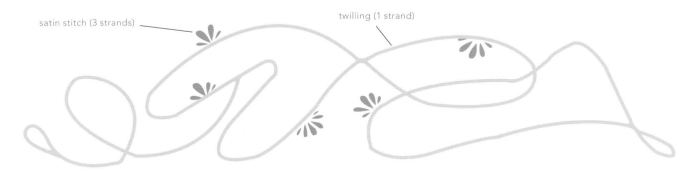

Color/stitching guide

3. Next, fold up the sides, right sides together, lining up the top. The bottom piece will be folded directly in half. Sew each side together (Figure 3).

4. Last, fold and tuck in each side of the bottom, forming a triangle on each side. Sew each triangle fold down (Figure 4).

5. Repeat steps 2–4 with your outer fabric for the outside of the bag.

6. To make the handles, place the outer fabric and the lining right sides together and sew down each side, leaving the ends open (Figure 5).

7. Turn the tube right sides out and press. Repeat steps 6–7 for the second handle.

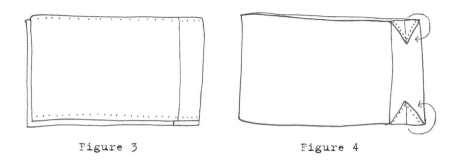

Figure 3   Figure 4

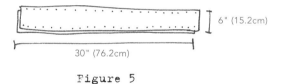

6" (15.2cm)

30" (76.2cm)

Figure 5

Template
Enlarge at 265%.

8. Make sure the outside of the bag is turned right side out and the lining of the bag is turned wrong side out. Insert the outside layer inside of the lining layer so that the right sides of each layer are facing each other.

Place one handle in between the layers on each side of the bag. The side of each handle will be 4" (10.2cm) from the side of the bag (Figure 6). Line up the top edges and pin in place, leaving an 8" (20.3cm) opening on one side.

9. Sew around the top of the bag, excluding the 8" (20.3cm) opening (Figure 7). You may want to reinforce the stitching in the handle seam allowances for needed strength.

10. Now you can pull the outside layer out through the opening and tuck the lining in.

11. Finish by slip stitching the opening closed (Figure 8).

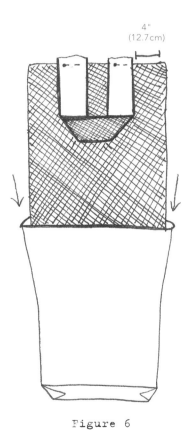

4"
(12.7cm)

Figure 6

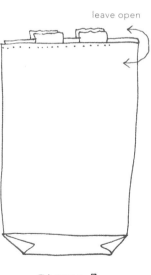

leave open

Figure 7

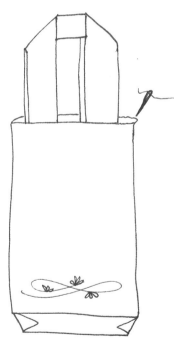

Figure 8

Itty Bitty Bedroom

BALANCED BABY crib quilt

FOXY CLOCK AND BUNNY TUBE framed art

CATCHING DREAMS crib mobile

PATCHED IN boy's pants

FAWNSIE FRIENDSHIP little girl's dress

Balanced Baby crib quilt

Oh, you sweet little pink-cheeked baby! You need the cutest room ever, and what better way to start than with a crib quilt? This one is a great mixture of sweet and cool. The simple color blocking allows you to focus on your favorite color while adding eye-catching graphic detail.

FINISHED SIZE

42" × 60" (106.7cm × 152.4cm)

FABRIC

Main print: 1½ yards (1.4m)

Secondary print: ⅝ yard (0.6m)

Solid: 1 yard (0.9m)

Backing: 54" × 72" (137.2cm × 182.9cm)

Binding: ½ yard (0.5m)

TECHNIQUES USED

Tracing (page 12)

Satin stitch (page 8)

Backstitch (page 8)

Needle-turn appliqué (page 12)

Quilting (page 12) and Binding (page 13)

SUPPLIES

Template (page 74)

Washable or iron-off fabric pen and light source

Lightweight tear-away stabilizer: 1 yard (0.9m)

5 colors of embroidery floss (shown, for baby girl quilt: DMC no. 831, no. 833, no. 933, no. 943, no. 991; suggested, for baby boy quilt: DMC no. 356, no. 680, no. 815, no. 834, no. 919)

Size 22 chenille needle

Small appliqué needle, for needle-turn appliqué

Batting: 54" × 72" (137.2cm × 182.9cm)

Pieced by Megan Frock
Quilted by Jessica Defibaugh

Cutting

From the main print, cut:
(5) 10" × 10" (25.4cm × 25.4cm)
(1) 32" × WOF (81.3cm × WOF)

From the secondary print, cut:
(1) 18" × WOF (45.7cm × WOF)

From the solid fabric, cut:
(1) 18" × WOF (45.7cm × WOF)
(1) 12" × WOF (30.5cm × WOF)

From the binding fabric, cut:
(5) 2½" × WOF (6.4cm × WOF)

From the stabilizer, cut:
(5) 10" × 10" (25.4cm × 25.4cm)

For both your solid 18" × WOF (45.7cm × WOF) and your 18" × WOF (45.7cm × WOF) secondary print, cut each in half and then cut each half from corner to corner on the diagonal. Keep only the two middle triangles from each fabric piece (Figure 1).

NOTE: Don't trash those leftover triangles! Save them in your scrap collection to use another day.

Sewing

NOTE: All seams are ¼" (6mm). Make sure you sew your fabric right sides together, and press your seams as you go.

1. Arrange the four triangles as shown in Figure 2. Sew them together two at a time, joining one solid and one print together at the longest side of the triangle, right sides together (Figure 3).

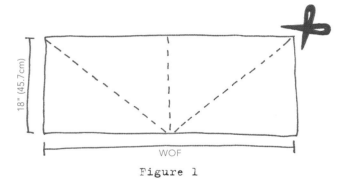

Figure 1

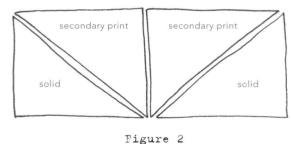

Figure 2

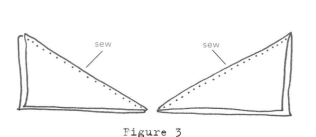

Figure 3

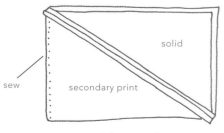

Figure 4

2. Once you have your 2 blocks, open them up and place them right sides together, lining up the 2 print sides, and sew the 2 blocks together where the prints meet (Figure 4). The print triangles should form a "V" when opened.

3. With your new pieced triangles forming a rectangle, you can now sew your 3 quilt pieces together. To do this, place one piece to the next with right sides together (Figure 5).

4. To finish, stitch around all 4 sides of the quilt—¼" (6mm) from the edge—to keep it from pulling apart during quilting.

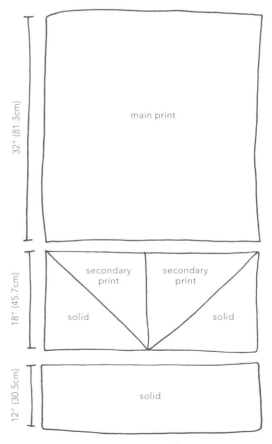

Figure 5

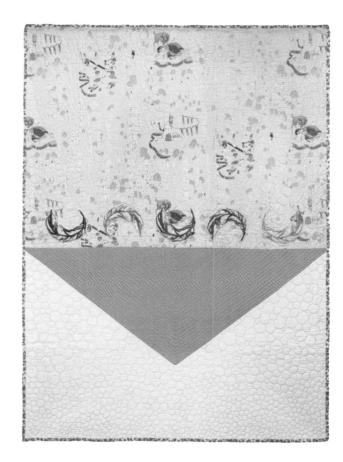

Figure 1

Figure 2

Embroidery

1. Using the template provided, trace 1 feather on each of your five 10" × 10" (25.4cm × 25.4cm) blocks, 3 facing right and 2 reversed to face left (Figure 1).

Template
Enlarge at 200%, 1 as is and 1 in reverse.

2. Before you begin stitching, place a piece of stabilizer under each fabric block, and safety pin each corner.

3. Embroider your design following the color/stitching guide. Each feather is one color. Repeat until all 5 blocks are complete. Once finished, tear off your stabilizer.

NOTE: Shown on the next page is a quilt/floss color guide for a baby boy version of this quilt as well.

Needle-turn appliqué

1. Before you get started, trim down each embroidered block, leaving ¼" (6mm) around each feather (Figure 2).

2. Once your feathers are trimmed, place them 1" (2.5cm) above the bottom of the main print, spacing them 2" (5.1cm) apart. This will leave roughly 4"

(10.2cm) from each side of the quilt (see finished quilt on page 73).

3. You can now needle-turn each feather onto your quilt.

Quilting and binding

Once your quilt top is completed, layer and quilt it as desired. Bind your quilt with the 2½" (6.4cm) wide fabric strips.

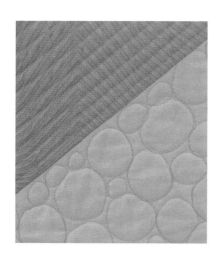

DMC floss colors (one per feather):

no. 991   no. 833   no. 943   no. 831   no. 933

DMC floss colors (one per feather):

no. 815   no. 834   no. 919   no. 680   no. 356

baby girl version

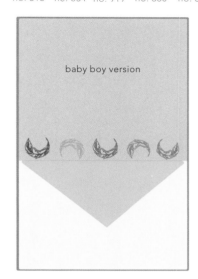

baby boy version

dashed lines: backstitch
(2 strands)

solid sections: satin stitch
(2 strands)

Color/stitching guide

Foxy Clock and Bunny Tube framed art

Time's a ticking and the channels are changing! What better way to make this precious time count than by making a sweet work of art for someone special? Hand-made art brings a feeling of warmth and love in a way that nothing else can. These fun prints work great together as well as separately.

FINISHED EMBROIDERY

9" × 6¾" (22.9cm × 17.1cm) for Bunny Tube, 6½" × 6½" (16.5cm × 16.5cm) for Foxy Clock

FABRIC

White linen: ⅓ yard (.3m) per design

4 printed fabrics: ¼ yard (.23m) each per design

Note: Keep in mind the direction of each fabric as you decide on patterns and amounts.

TECHNIQUES USED

Tracing (page 12)

Satin stitch (page 8)

Backstitch (page 8)

Running stitch (page 8)

French knot (page 9)

SUPPLIES

Templates (page 79)

Washable or iron-off fabric pen and light source

Lightweight tear-away stabilizer: 10¼" × 12¼" (26cm × 31.1cm) per design

Embroidery floss: 11 colors for Bunny Tube (shown: DMC no. 310, no. 349, no. 351, no. 400, no. 822, no. 833, no. 954, no. 3779, no. 3851, no. 4040/variegated, no. 4130/variegated) or 7 colors for Foxy Clock (shown: DMC no. 310, no. 349, no. 400, no. 747, no. 822, no. 833, no. 4130/variegated)

Size 22 chenille needle

Frame: 16" × 20" (40.6cm × 50.8cm) per design

White cardboard, cut to size of inside edge of frame

Adhesive tape

Cutting

NOTE: The instructions that follow are for making one design.

From the white linen, cut:
(1) 10¼" × 12¼" (26cm × 31.1cm)

From 2 of the prints, cut:
(1) 6" × 10¼" (15.2cm × 26cm) from each. These are the top and bottom pieces.

From the 2 remaining prints, cut:
(1) 5" × 23" (12.7cm × 58.4cm) from each. These are the side pieces.

Embroidery

1. Begin by tracing your chosen template onto your white linen.

2. Once traced, place the linen right side up directly on top of your stabilizer and place a safety pin in each corner to secure it.

3. Now you can stitch, following the color/stitching guide for your design. Once finished, tear excess stabilizer off from around the design.

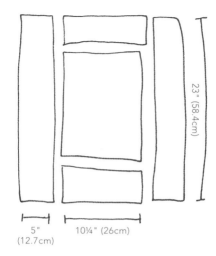

5"
(12.7cm)   10¼" (26cm)   23" (58.4cm)

Figure 1

Sewing

NOTE: Do not iron over light-weight stabilizer because it will melt onto your iron if it comes directly into contact with it. To iron your embroidery, place a scrap piece of fabric over the design and press gently.

All seams are ¼" (6mm), and always remember to place right sides together.

1. To piece your art together, attach one of your short pieces of fabric to the top of your white linen, lining up the 10¼" (26cm) sides (right sides together). Pin in place and sew. Repeat for your bottom piece. Press.

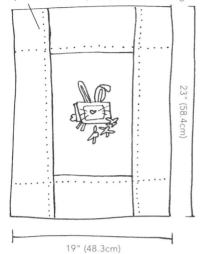

topstitch lines ¼" (6mm) from inside edges

23" (58.4cm)

19" (48.3cm)

Figure 2

2. Add one long strip on each side, lining up the 23" (58.4cm) sides. Pin in place and sew in the same manner as you used on the top and bottom pieces. Refer to Figure 1 for the layout.

3. Once everything is sewn in place, give it a good pressing.

4. Lastly, top stitch a few lines on top of the block, ¼" (6mm) from each seam (Figure 2). NOTE: Top stitching is simply a decorative line of stitching sewn on top of the right side of a project to give it a finished look.

Foxy Clock template
Enlarge at 200%.

Framing

All done! Now you can frame
your cute little art. When framing
fabric, I like to cut a piece of white
cardboard to the size of the inside
edge of the frame, center the design and fold the sides around the
edges of the cardboard. Secure it
tautly in place with adhesive tape.

Bunny Tube template
Enlarge at 200%.

DMC floss colors:

no. 822　no. 747　no. 833　no. 349　no. 4130　no. 400　no. 310

all solid areas:
satin stitch
(3 strands)

whisker dots:
French knots
(3 strands)

dashed lines:
running stitch
(6 strands)

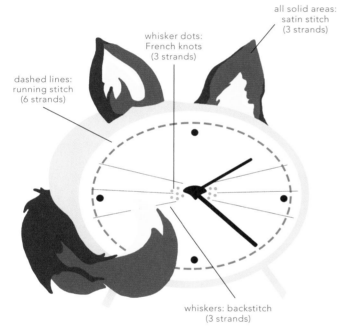

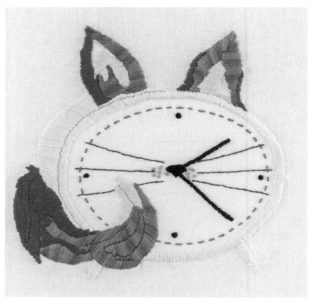

whiskers: backstitch
(3 strands)

Color/stitching guide

DMC floss colors:

no. 822 no. 4040 no. 954 no. 3851 no. 4130 no. 3779 no. 351 no. 349 no. 833 no. 400 no. 310

ears (lines only) and whiskers:
backstitch (3 strands)

dashed lines:
running stitch
(6 strands)

flower centers:
French knots
(6 strands)

all solid areas: satin stitch
(3 strands)

Color/stitching guide

Catching Dreams crib mobile

A crib mobile is essential in a nursery. This design is simple and clean, with focus on the charms. They're the most important part, right? A glimpse of their colors and shapes is sure to stimulate baby's senses and makes for an amazing dreamland!

FINISHED SIZE
36" × 21" (91.4cm × 53.3cm)

FABRIC
2 prints: 14" × 14" (35.6cm × 35.6cm) each

Linen: ¼ yard (0.23m)

TECHNIQUES USED
Tracing (page 12) or Transferring (page 12)

Couched filling stitch (page 9)

SUPPLIES
Template (page 84)

Fusible fleece: ⅜ yard (.34m)

Washable or iron-off fabric pen and light source

4 colors of embroidery floss that coordinate with your print fabric

Size 22 chenille needle

Small cording or twine: 4½ yards (4.1m)

Dowel rod: ⅞" × 21" (22mm × 53.3cm)

Optional: Acrylic craft paint (gold shown)

½" (13mm) cording: 4½ yards (4.1m)

Hot glue gun or craft glue

Cutting

Using the circle template, cut:
2 from each print
4 from the linen
8 from the fusible fleece

From the small cording or twine, cut:
(4) 25" (63.5cm)
(1) 55" (139.7cm)

Embroidery

1. Once your cutting is done, iron the wrong side of each fabric circle to a circle of fusible fleece.

2. Trace the grid template onto the center of each linen circle (Figure 1).

3. To embroider, follow the stitching guide, using a different floss color for each mobile circle. (Choose floss colors that complement your print fabric choices.)

Sewing

1. Once all of your handwork is finished, you can sew your circle charms. Place one linen embroidered circle and one print circle wrong sides together. Fold up the bottom 2" (5.1cm) of a piece of your cut twine and place it in between the two circles.

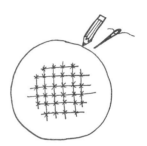

Figure 1

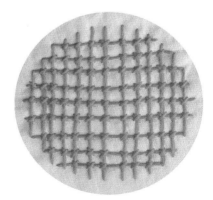

Stitching guide
All stitches are couched filling (3 strands).

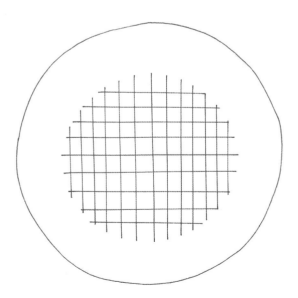

Template and grid
Enlarge 200%.

2. Next, using a ⅜" (10mm) seam, sew the two circles together, leaving the edges raw (Figure 2). Trim the little piece of twine off.

3. Repeat steps 1–2 for the next three circle charms.

NOTE: To achieve a more raveled look, you may wash and dry your charms.

Constructing your mobile

1. Paint each end of your rod (they will show) if desired (I used gold), or leave the wood as is.

2. Mark 4 points on your dowel rod from left to right at 6½" (16.5cm), 9" (22.9cm), 12" (30.5cm) and 14" (35.6cm). Each mark represents where a charm will hang.

3. Each piece of twine that is attached to a charm will be wrapped once around the dowel and glued into place. The excess twine should be cut off. From left to right and measuring only the twine (not the charm), the first charm should hang 12" (30.5cm) long; the second, 6½" (16.5cm); the third, 18" (45.7cm); and the fourth, 11½" (29.2cm).

4. Once all charms are hung and glued, use your 55" (139.7cm) twine to create a hanger. Place both ends at the center of the dowel rod and glue in place. Stretch the twine out and glue at each end of the rod, but not on the side of the ends (Figure 3).

5. Take your ½" (13mm) cording and wrap it around the dowel rod, securing it with glue as you go along (Figure 4). The cording should cover all of your unsightly twine.

Now find a cute little hook and hang your sweet mobile up!

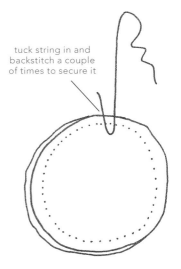

tuck string in and backstitch a couple of times to secure it

Figure 2

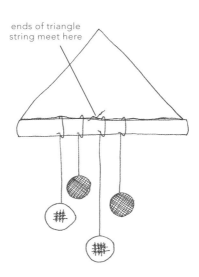

ends of triangle string meet here

Figure 3

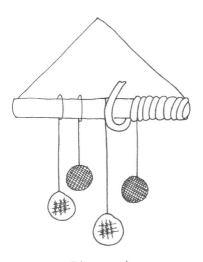

Figure 4

Patched In boy's pants

Only the coolest kids get patched in! Appliqué is one of the easiest ways to add style to store-bought clothes. Warning: Sewing on these cute knee patches just might make your little guy lightning fast.

FINISHED PATCH

3½" (8.9cm) round, shown on size 2T pants

FABRIC

Store-bought pair of pants, any size for baby or toddler

3 fabric scraps: 5" × 5" (12.7cm × 12.7cm) each

TECHNIQUES USED

Appliqué (page 12)

Blanket stitch (page 8)

SUPPLIES

Templates (page 89)

Fusible web: 18" × 18" (45.7cm × 45.7cm)

Washable or iron-off fabric pen and light source

2 colors of embroidery floss (shown: DMC no. 165, no. 816)

Size 22 chenille needle

Appliqué and embroidery

1. Begin by ironing your fusible web to the wrong side of the fabric scraps, then cut out your appliqué pieces using the templates provided. Cut 2 of each circle from two of the scraps. Cut 1 of each lightning bolt from the last scrap.

2. Peel off the paper backing from your appliqué pieces one at a time as you layer and iron the pieces together in the order shown (Figure 1). Then iron each completed circle to the knees of the pants (Figure 2).

3. Add embroidery to the appliqué following the color/stitching guide.

NOTE: These patches would also look great on the back pockets.

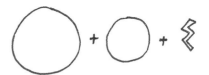

Figure 1

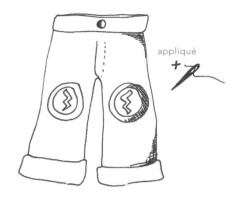

appliqué

Figure 2

DMC floss colors:

no. 816   no. 165

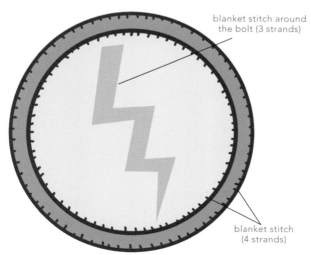

blanket stitch around the bolt (3 strands)

blanket stitch (4 strands)

Color/stitching guide

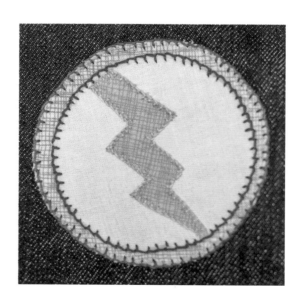

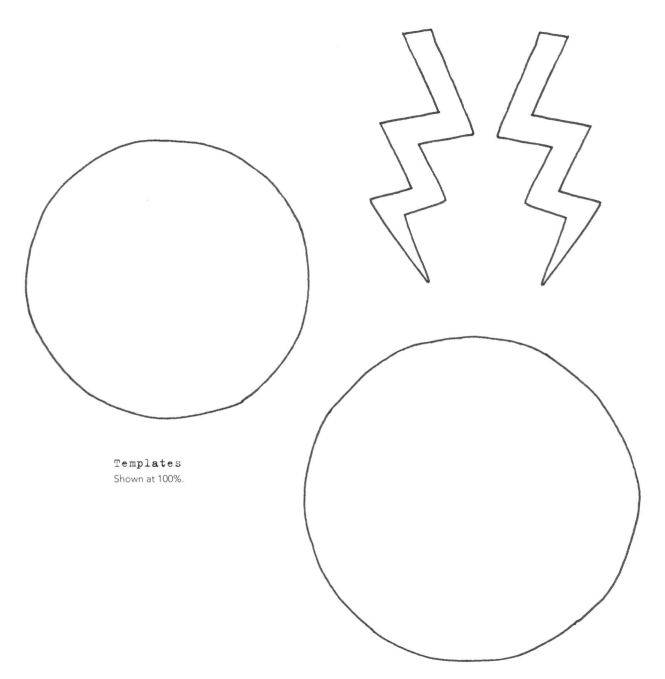

Templates
Shown at 100%.

Fawnsie Friendship
little girl's dress

- -

What's sweeter than a cute little gal in a frock?
Two little fawns whose friendship grows in a field of
flowers! This sweet appliqué is a great addition to any
dress. I only hope you can stand the cuteness.

FINISHED EMBROIDERY/APPLIQUÉ

3½" × 5½" (8.9cm × 14cm),
shown on size 12–18 months dress

FABRIC

Store-bought dress, any size for baby
or toddler

1 fabric scrap: 7" × 7" (17.8cm × 17.8cm)

TECHNIQUES USED

Appliqué (page 12)

Blanket stitch (page 8)

Lazy daisy stitch (page 9)

SUPPLIES

Templates (page 93)

Fusible web: 7" × 7" (17.8cm × 17.8cm)

Washable or iron-off fabric pen and light source

2 colors of embroidery floss (shown: DMC no. 307,
no. 754)

Small appliqué needle

Appliqué and embroidery

1. Begin by ironing your fusible web to the wrong side of the fabric scrap, then cut out your fawns using the template provided.

2. Peel off the paper backing, then iron each appliqué piece to the dress.

NOTE: On this dress, the design is placed off to one side along the bottom (Figure 1), but choose a location that works best with your dress.

3. Once your fawns are ironed on, place and trace the flower template over it.

4. Stitch around the appliqué and embroider the flowers following the color/stitching guide.

DMC floss colors:

no. 754   no. 307

Color/stitching guide

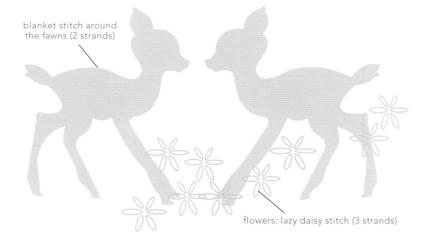

blanket stitch around
the fawns (2 strands)

flowers: lazy daisy stitch (3 strands)

Figure 1

Template and flower guide
Shown at 100%.

4

Big Kid's Crib

JAMS twin quilt

TELLIN' TIME activity pillow

ELECTRO SLIDE mini robe

RIGHT WAY napping bed

CALL ME SKETCH art backpack

Jams twin quilt

What's a beboppin' quilt without music? Not much when you're a preteen! As step-mom to a 9-year-old who owns three iPods and frequents the couch, this quilt is an essential. Shouldn't the "too cool" kid have a unique quilt? I think yes, plus it keeps the chocolate chip cookie stains off your quilt!

FINISHED SIZE

Twin, 58" × 88" (147.3cm × 223.5cm)

FABRIC

Light tan: 1½ yards (1.4m)

Light gray: ¾ yard (0.7m)

Dark gray: 1 yard (0.9m)

Cream: 1¼ yards (1.1m)

54" (137.2cm) natural-colored linen: ¾ yard (0.7m)

54" (137.2cm) white linen: ½ yard (0.5m)

White cotton: 1⅞ yards (1.7m)

Backing: 70" × 100" (177.8cm × 254cm)

Binding: ⅝ yard (0.6m)

Pieced by Megan Frock
Quilted by Jessica Defibaugh

TECHNIQUES USED

Tracing (page 12) or Transferring (page 12)

Satin stitch (page 8)

Backstitch (page 8)

Running stitch (page 8)

Whipped running stitch (page 8)

Quilting (page 12) and Binding (page 13)

SUPPLIES

Template (page 103)

Tracing or transferring supplies

Lightweight tear-away stabilizer: 12" × 16" (30.5cm × 40.6cm)

9 colors of embroidery floss (shown: DMC no. 309, no. 891, no. 894, no. 945, no. 955, no. 963, no. 3706, no. 3851, ecru)

Size 22 chenille needle

Batting: 70" × 100" (177.8cm × 254cm)

Cutting

From the white cotton, cut:
(2) 11" × 11" (27.9cm × 27.9cm)
(28) 8" × 8" (20.3cm × 20.3cm)

From the cream fabric, cut:
(2) 11" × 11" (27.9cm × 27.9cm)
(14) 8" × 8" (20.3cm × 20.3cm)

From the light tan fabric, cut:
(29) 8" × 8" (20.3cm × 20.3cm)

From the light gray fabric, cut:
(6) 8" × 8" (20.3cm × 20.3cm)

From the dark gray fabric, cut:
(19) 8" × 8" (20.3cm × 20.3cm)

From the white linen, cut:
(7) 8" × 8" (20.3cm × 20.3cm)

From the natural-colored linen, cut:
(14) 8" × 8" (20.3cm × 20.3cm)

From the binding fabric, cut:
(7) 2½" × WOF (6.4cm × WOF)

Now that all of your fabrics are cut into squares, cut them into triangles as follows: from each 8" (20.3cm) square, you will get 4 triangles by cutting diagonally from corner to corner twice (Figure 1).

Next, cut the four 11" (27.9cm) squares in the same manner as the 8" (20.3cm) squares (Figure 2).

Figure 1

Figure 2

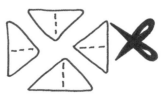

Figure 3

Now that the 11" (27.9cm) squares are cut into triangles, cut each of those triangles in half. This will leave you with 8 triangles from each 11" (27.9cm) square (Figure 3).

Sewing

NOTE: All seams are ¼" (6mm). Be sure to sew your fabric right sides together, and press the seams as you go.

FABRIC KEY: From this point on in some of the illustrations, your fabrics will be assigned a letter according to color to keep them in order:
T = Light tan
C = Cream
N = Natural linen
WL = White linen
WC = White cotton
LG = Light gray
DG = Dark gray
M = Mixed

1. Using the triangles from your 11" (27.9cm) squares, you will sew 4 blocks. Begin by laying out the triangles (Figure 4).

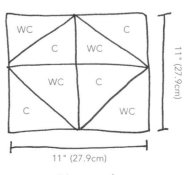

Figure 4

Figure 5

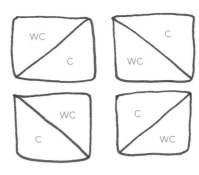

Figure 6

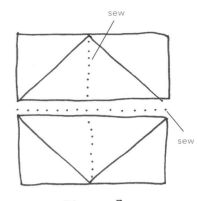

Figure 7

2. Once your triangles are ordered correctly, begin sewing them together to form your blocks. To do this, first sew the long edges of two triangles right sides together to form one piece (Figure 5). Repeat until you have 4 sewn pieces. (Be careful not to stretch or tug your fabrics as you piece them together.) Then refer to Figures 6 and 7 for sewing each piece to the next. Repeat until all 4 blocks are complete.

3. Now that you have your 4 new blocks, trim them down 1½" (3.8cm) on each side to 8" (20.3cm) blocks. Don't worry about preserving points; just focus on getting an 8" (20.3cm) square.

4. Next, cut each new block into 4 new triangles (Figures 8 and 9).

Piecing your quilt

Now that you have loads of triangles, you can begin sewing the rows of your quilt. Each of your 26 rows will consist of 18 triangles. Here's where the fabric key will come in handy.

NOTE: The pieced triangles sewn in the previous steps will now be referred to as your mixed triangles (M = mixed).

1. Refer to Figure 10 for row layouts. For each row, the first triangle's point will point up and the last will point down. I would suggest only laying out two or three rows at a time and gradually working your way down, sewing the finished rows together as you go.

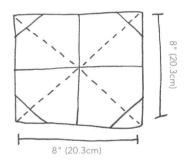

Figure 8

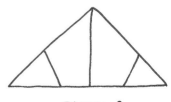

Figure 9

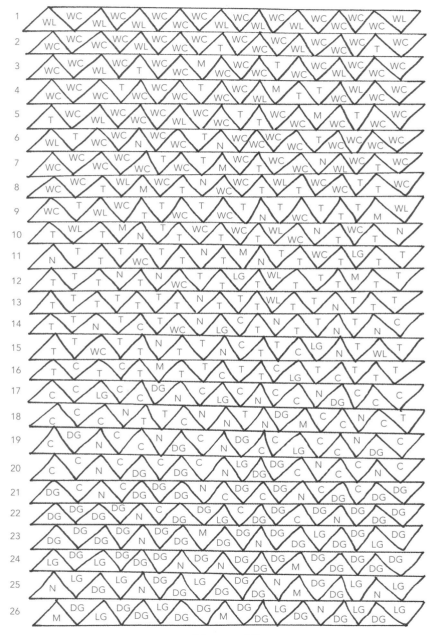

Figure 10

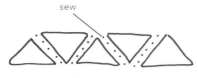

sew

Figure 11

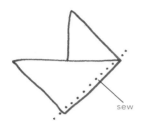

sew

Figure 12

Sew each triangle to the next by lining up the edges and keeping right sides together (Figures 11 and 12). Be sure the first and last triangle of each row are always facing the same direction as the previous row.

2. Once all of your rows are sewn, cut the "half triangles" off of the sides and square up your quilt.

3. Finish by sewing a quick stitch around all 4 sides, ¼" (6mm) from the edge. This will keep your pieces from separating during the quilting process.

Tracing and embroidery

NOTE: Before tracing or transferring the template, keep in mind that a quilt, once quilted, bound and washed, will shrink roughly 1–2 inches (2.5cm to 5.1cm). Do not place the embroidery too close to the edges.

1. Trace or transfer your embroidery design onto the bottom right corner of your quilt, about 6" (15.2cm) from the right edge and 6" (15.2cm) from the bottom edge (see finished quilt).

2. Once the design is traced or transferred onto your quilt, place your piece of stabilizer on the wrong side of the quilt, securing with a safety pin in each corner.

3. Embroider your design on the quilt, following the color/stitching guide.

Quilting and binding

Once your quilt top is completed, layer and quilt it as desired. Bind your quilt with the 2½" (6.4cm) wide fabric strips.

DMC floss colors:

no. 3851   no. 945   no. 955   no. 309   no. 891   no. 3706   no. 894   no. 963   ecru

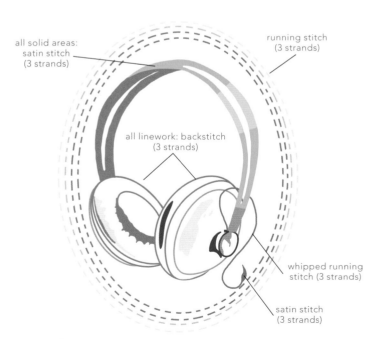

all solid areas: satin stitch (3 strands)

running stitch (3 strands)

all linework: backstitch (3 strands)

whipped running stitch (3 strands)

satin stitch (3 strands)

Color/stitching guide

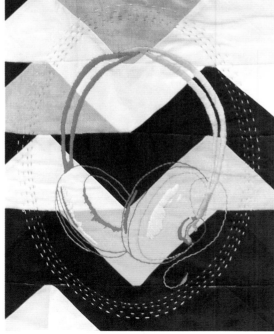

Template
Enlarge at 185%.

Tellin' Time activity pillow

Learning to tell time can be tough! Children respond greatly to visual learning aids, so why not have a giant, brightly colored clock pillow? The hands can turn to any time and the numbers are easy to read.

FINISHED SIZE

22" (55.9cm) round

FABRIC

Print for appliqué and sides: 1 yard (0.9m)

Print for piping: ¼ yard (.2m)

54" (137.2cm) WOF linen: ¾ yard (.7m), or 1½ yards (1.4m) if your fabric is 45" (114.3cm) wide

Felted wool: 11" × 13" (27.9cm × 33cm)

TECHNIQUES USED

Appliqué (page 12)

Blanket stitch (page 8)

Slip stitch (page 9)

Single buttonhole bar stitch (page 9)

SUPPLIES

Templates (page 109)

Round plate

Washable or iron-off fabric pen

Fusible web, at least 25" (63.5cm) wide: ¾ yard (.7m)

1 color of embroidery floss (shown: DMC no. 3023)

Appliqué needle

Fusible fleece: 1½ yards (1.4m)

Batting (tightly woven): 7" × 39" (17.8cm × 99.1cm)

³⁄₁₆" (5mm) Wrap 'n Fuse or ready-made piping: 4⅛ yards (3.8m)

Zipper foot for sewing machine

Stuffing

Two 1½" (3.8cm) covered buttons

Upholstery needle

Cutting

From the linen, cut:
(2) 25" × 25" (63.5cm × 63.5cm)

From the batting, cut:
(2) 3½" × 39" (8.9cm × 99.1cm)

From the print for the piping, cut:
(4) 1½" × WOF (3.8cm × WOF)
strips

From the felted wool, using the
templates, cut 1 big clock hand,
1 small clock hand and numbers
1 through 12. The best way to cut
the wool is to pin on copies of the
templates and cut around them.

From the print for the sides and
appliqué, cut:
(2) 3" × 37" (7.6cm × 94cm)
(1) 25" × 25" (63.5cm × 63.5cm)

Next, out of your 25" (63.5cm)
print square, you will cut two circles for the appliqué. Cut 1 piece
of fusible web 25" (63.5cm) square.
Begin by measuring 12½" (31.8cm)
over and 12½" (31.8cm) down to
find the center of the web, then
mark it. Next, find the center of
each side and mark them as well.

Using your center and side marks,
draw both a horizontal and vertical
line across the web. Next, draw a
line from corner to corner twice,

forming an X. Using your new
lines, you will measure out and
mark 4 points on each line. Starting from your center point, you
will mark each line at 1½" (3.8cm),
6" (15.2cm), 9" (22.9cm) and 10½"
(26.7cm) (Figure 1).

Once all of your points are
marked, you can connect the dots
to form 4 circles. Using a plate or
round object can help you achieve
a nice curve. Fuse the web to the
back of the 25" (63.5cm) print
square. Cut the circles out.

Appliqué

1. Begin by laying out one of
your 25" (63.5cm) linen squares to
appliqué on. Fuse your 2 circles
onto the center.

2. Next, place your numbers,
spacing them evenly between the
two circles. Because the numbers
are felted wool, you won't need
fusible web. You can simply pin
them in place (Figure 2).

3. Stitch around all appliqué,
including circles and numbers,
using 2 strands of floss and a
blanket stitch.

4. Once your appliqué is complete, trim down, leaving ½"
(13mm) around the outside circle

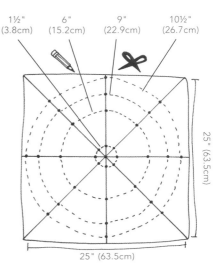

Figure 1

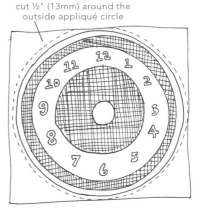

cut ½" (13mm) around the
outside appliqué circle

Figure 2

as shown in Figure 2. Using this
circle as a template, cut the second 25" (63.5cm) linen square into
a matching circle.

5. On the wrong side of each of
the two linen circles, apply your
fusible fleece and trim off the
excess.

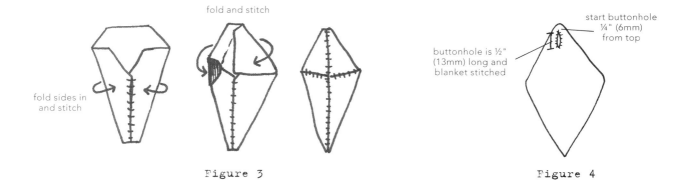

fold and stitch

fold sides in
and stitch

Figure 3

start buttonhole
¼" (6mm)
from top

buttonhole is ½"
(13mm) long and
blanket stitched

Figure 4

Constructing the clock hands

1. To construct the clock hands, you will need the two pieces cut earlier from your templates. Each hand uses the same method of folding and hand stitching (Figure 3). You will use 2 strands of floss and a slip stitch. Make sure your stitch is fairly tight to hold the felted wool together.

2. After each hand is finished, add a ½" (13mm) long buttonhole ¼" (6mm) from the top point of each one. To do this, make a mark with a fabric pen and cut a slit (Figure 4). Once your hole is cut, use a single buttonhole bar stitch and 2 strands of floss to finish it off.

Constructing the pillow sides

Place your 2 side fabric pieces right sides together and sew at one short end to form one long piece. Repeat this process with your batting pieces.

2. Place your fabric right side up on top of your batting, and quilt (Figure 5).

NOTE: A project as small as this is super-easy to quilt on your home machine. You don't need any special tools. Simple straight lines are the easiest. Practice on a piece of scrap fabric to perfect your skills.

Piping

1. Begin by sewing all of your 1½" (3.8cm) strips together to form one long strip by sewing right sides together at the short ends.

2. Next, lay out the fabric strip and piping (wrong side of fabric toward the piping). With Wrap 'n Fuse piping, you simply iron the fabric snugly around the piping, following the manufacturer's instructions. Leave 2" (5.1cm) of extra fabric at one end.

NOTE: You can also purchase ready-made piping at most craft stores if you wish.

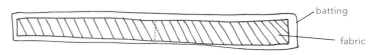

batting

fabric

Figure 5

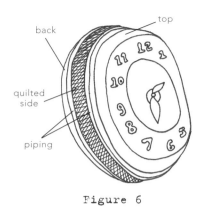

Figure 6

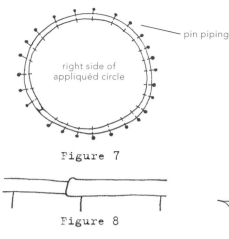

Figure 7

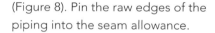

Figure 8

Figure 9

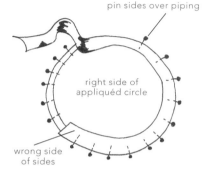

Figure 10

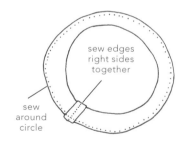

Figure 11

Figure 12

Constructing the pillow

NOTE: Refer to Figure 6 for the overall layout.

1. Begin by laying out the front circle, right side up. Next, lay the piping around the circle, aligning all raw edges and pinning in place (Figure 7). The right side of the piping will face the inside of the circle, and the flat side will face the outside edges. Do not cut your piping to size yet.

2. Now you need to merge your two piping ends. Fold the end with the extra 2" (5.1cm) of fabric under 1" (2.5cm). Trim the un-folded end until it fits perfectly up against the inside of the folded pocket. Placing the folded side over the opposite end of the pip-ing will form one continuous tube

(Figure 8). Pin the raw edges of the piping into the seam allowance.

3. Now that the piping is pinned down, place the side piece around the circle, with its right side fac-ing the right side of the circle. Leave each end of your side piece 1" (2.5cm) longer and pull the two ends right sides together. Mark where they meet and sew a straight stitch (Figure 9).

4. After stitching, align the sides back up with the circle as you did previously and pin. You will use the same pins, just pull them out one at a time and reinsert to hold both the piping and the side (Figure 10).

5. Next, sew around the circle us-ing a zipper foot to accommodate the piping (Figure 11). You will want the stitch to be snug up to the piping.

6. Once the top is sewn to the side, repeat the process to attach the bottom circle and piping to the side as well (Figure 12). Leave a 5" (12.7cm) opening, fill with stuffing and slip stitch closed, being sure to catch in all the layers.

7. Cover your two buttons with a piece of linen, following the button manufacturer's instructions.

8. After your two buttons are covered, line up the top button, big-hand buttonhole and small-hand buttonhole with the back button (Figure 13). Use 6 strands of floss and your upholstery needle to attach the buttons. Start by tying the end of the thread to the top button, and then thread through the buttonholes and the center of the pillow top, coming out at the center back. Once the thread is through, pull it taut and tie it to the back button.

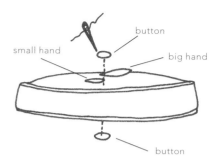

Figure 13

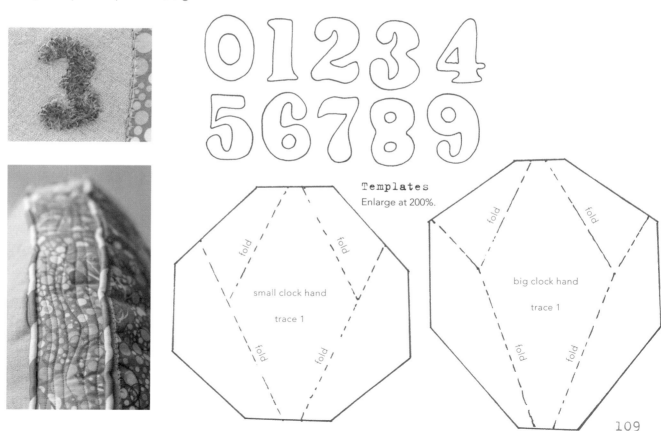

Templates
Enlarge at 200%.

small clock hand

trace 1

big clock hand

trace 1

109

Electro Slide mini robe

Sleepover time, bath time, lounge time: Any time is a good time for a mini robe! A little robe with a little robot love is sure to make your wee one feel special. You can buy any robe and instantly transform it into a one-of-a-kind garment for your very own cuddle bug.

FINISHED EMBROIDERY

8" × 4¼" (20.3cm × 10.8cm), shown on youth size 8 diamond waffle-weave spa robe

FABRIC

Store-bought robe, any size for child

1 fabric scrap: 7" × 7" (17.8cm × 17.8cm)

TECHNIQUES USED

Tracing (page 12) or Transferring (page 12)

Appliqué (page 12)

Backstitch (page 8)

Blanket stitch (page 8)

Satin stitch (page 8)

Running stitch (page 8)

SUPPLIES

Templates (page 112)

Washable or iron-off fabric pen and light source or transfer supplies

Fusible web: 7" × 7" (17.8cm × 17.8cm)

3–4 colors of embroidery floss (shown, for boy robot: DMC no. 310, no. 321, no. 729; suggested, for girl robot: DMC no. 310, no. 353, no. 718, no. 3802)

Size 22 chenille needle

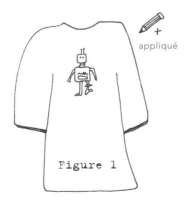

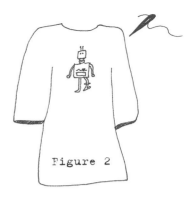

Appliqué and design

1. Begin by tracing or transferring the robot design onto the back of the robe (Figure 1). I like to center the design between the neckline and belt.

NOTE: If the robe is a thick material, it is better to use a transfer pen or transfer paper instead of a light source. If this is the case, remember to trace the design backwards.

2. Iron the fusible web to your fabric scrap, then cut out the appliqué pieces (the robot head and body) and apply them on top of the existing design on the robe (Figure 2). (The appliqué templates are already shown

backwards because you will trace the design onto the fusible web's paper backing and not the fabric.)

3. Once your appliqué pieces are on you will need to retrace the embroidery that lies on top of the appliqué.

+
appliqué

Figure 1

Figure 2

Templates
Enlarge at 200%. Leave out the heart and line for the boy robot version.

Embroidery

Embroider your design following the color/stitching guide, and add blanket stitching around the appliquéd robot head and body.

NOTE: Shown are color/stitching guides for both girl and boy robot versions.

DMC floss colors:

no. 353   no. 718   no. 3802   no. 310

DMC floss colors:

no. 729   no. 321   no. 310

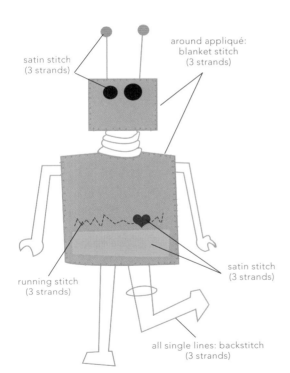

satin stitch (3 strands)

around appliqué: blanket stitch (3 strands)

satin stitch (3 strands)

running stitch (3 strands)

all single lines: backstitch (3 strands)

Color/stitching guide (girl robot)

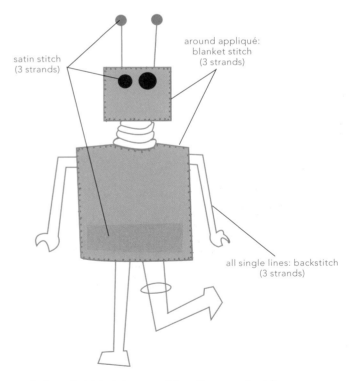

satin stitch (3 strands)

around appliqué: blanket stitch (3 strands)

all single lines: backstitch (3 strands)

Color/stitching guide (boy robot)

Right Way napping bed

Sleepover! How exciting! There are several sleepover essentials, but the most important one has got to be a sleeping bag. This project is essentially a quilt-turned-napping bed. Because it has cushioning made with three full-size pillows, it is super-comfy, and the quilted half is big enough to provide plenty of covers.

FINISHED SIZE

66" × 71" (167.6cm × 180.3cm), open

FABRIC

Main print: 1¼ yards (1.1m)

Secondary print: ⅔ yard (.6m)

Accent: 1⅞ yards (1.7m)

Arrow: ½ yard (.5m)

Backing (flannel or velveteen): 78" × 83" (198.1cm × 210.8cm)

Binding: ½ yard (0.5m)

Note: Fabric requirements may need to be increased if your fabric is directional.

TECHNIQUES USED

Appliqué (page 12)

Various stitches (page 8)

Quilting (page 12) and Binding (page 13)

SUPPLIES

Fusible web: ⅔ yard (.6m)

Washable or iron-off fabric pen

1 color of embroidery floss (shown: DMC no. 310)

Size 22 chenille needle

Batting: 78" × 83" (198.1cm × 210.8cm)

3 standard-size bed pillows

Pieced by Megan Frock
Quilted by Jessica Defibaugh

Cutting

From the main print, cut:
(1) 44" × WOF (111.8cm × WOF)

From the secondary print, cut:
(1) 22½" × WOF (57.2cm × WOF)

From the accent fabric, cut:
(1) 28" × 66" (71.1cm × 167.6cm)

From the arrow fabric, cut:
(1) 9" × 13" (22.9cm × 33cm)
(1) 13" × 19" (33cm × 48.3cm)

From the binding fabric, cut:
(7) 2½" × WOF (6.4cm × WOF)

Sewing

NOTE: All seams are ¼" (6mm). Make sure you sew your fabric right sides together and press as you sew.

1. Begin by placing your main and second main prints together at the WOF end (Figure 1).

2. Next, attach your accent fabric as shown in Figure 2.

Appliqué

1. Cut your 13" × 19" (33cm × 48.3cm) arrow piece in half diagonally (Figure 3). Keep one triangle and discard the other.

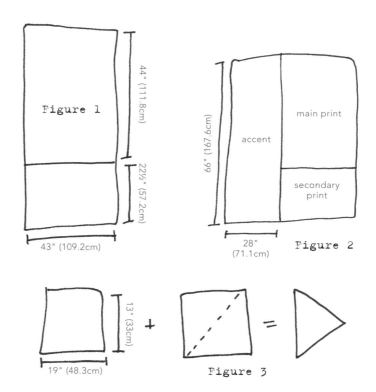

Figure 1

Figure 2

Figure 3

2. Back your two arrow pieces with fusible web and iron them onto your pieced top. The arrow will be placed 2½" (6.4cm) over from the seam and 11" (27.9cm) up from the bottom (Figure 4).

3. With 6 strands of floss, stitch around your arrow using what I call "Frankenstein" stitches—basically, several different stitches in any order and placement you'd like (Figure 5). This is a great time to get the kids involved for random stitching.

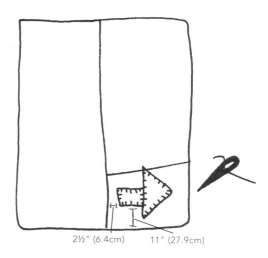

Figure 4

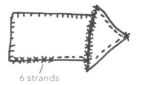

6 strands

Figure 5

Quilting

NOTE: You will use batting throughout the entire piece. Remember, your backing and batting should be 3"–6" (7.6cm to 15.2cm) bigger around all sides. If you are using a long arm quilter, provide the illustration (Figure 6).

1. Layer with batting and backing, then baste if desired.

2. On the left, add 4 lines following the measurements (Figure 6).

Draw them on with a washable or iron-off fabric pen before you begin quilting.

3. Stitch in the ditch on the seam that splits your fabrics down the middle. On the right side, quilt with an overall pattern. Once quilted, trim the excess.

Binding

With the 2½" (6.4cm) wide fabric strips, begin by binding only the top, bottom and right side. Once the binding is attached, insert your three pillows into their slots, pin the remaining binding in place, and finish attaching your binding by machine (Figure 7). Once all the binding is on, you can hand-stitch it to the back.

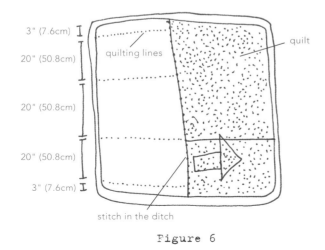

3" (7.6cm)

20" (50.8cm)

20" (50.8cm)

20" (50.8cm)

3" (7.6cm)

quilting lines

quilt

stitch in the ditch

Figure 6

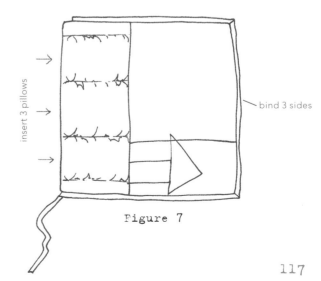

insert 3 pillows

bind 3 sides

Figure 7

Call Me Sketch art backpack

As an artist, I know how special your art supplies can be. As a child, I wanted a place for all of my art stuff. This bag is a great on-the-go carrier for drawing pads and tools. It is double-lined for extra strength. The wraparound tie will make any little artist feel as though they are opening a treasure every time they go to show off their creations!

FINISHED SIZE

20" × 16" (50.8cm × 40.6cm), closed

FABRIC

Main print: 1¼" yards (1.1m)

White linen: 1 yard (0.9m)

TECHNIQUES USED

Tracing (page 12) or Transferring (page 12)

Satin stitch (page 8)

Backstitch (page 8)

Slip stitch (page 9)

SUPPLIES

Template (page 121)

Washable or iron-off fabric pen and light source

Lightweight tear-away stabilizer: 7" × 11" (17.8cm × 27.9cm)

¼" (6mm) cording: 3 yards (2.7m)

2 colors of embroidery floss (shown: DMC no. 892, Metallic no. E3821)

Size 22 chenille needle

4 D-rings

Fusible fleece: 2¾ yards (2.5m)

DMC floss colors:

no. 892 no. E3821

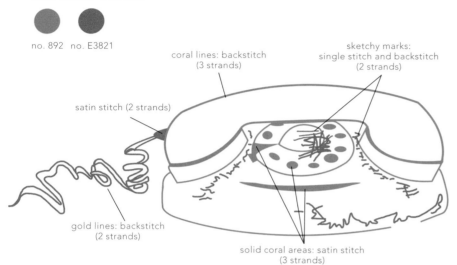

coral lines: backstitch
(3 strands)

sketchy marks:
single stitch and backstitch
(2 strands)

satin stitch (2 strands)

gold lines: backstitch
(2 strands)

solid coral areas: satin stitch
(3 strands)

Color/stitching guide

Cutting

From the main print, cut:
(2) 14" × 17" (35.6cm × 43.2cm)
(1) 17" × 23" (43.2cm × 58.4cm)
(2) 4" × 36" (10.2cm × 91.4cm)

From the white linen, cut:
(1) 14" × 17" (35.6cm × 43.2cm)
(1) 17" × 41½" (43.2cm × 105.4cm)

From the fusible fleece, cut:
(2) 17" × 41½" (43.2cm × 105.4cm)
(1) 11½" × 16½" (29.2cm × 41.9cm)

Piecing and embroidery

NOTE: All seams are ¼" (6mm) unless noted. Remember to always place right sides together, and press as you go.

1. Begin by constructing the outside of the bag. Place the two 17" (43.2cm) ends of the 14" × 17" (35.6cm × 43.2cm) main print pieces on either side of the two 17" (43.2cm) ends of the 14" × 17" (35.6cm × 43.2cm) white linen and sew them to the linen as shown in Figure 1.

2. Once finished, fold directly in half, lining up the two main print

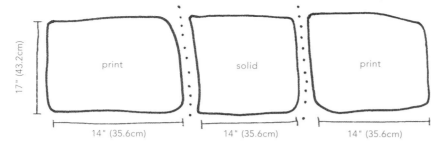

17" (43.2cm)

print   solid   print

14" (35.6cm)   14" (35.6cm)   14" (35.6cm)

Figure 1

pieces (wrong sides together). Your white linen will become the bottom of your bag. Press the fold on the linen to create a crisp line. This is the piece you will embroider.

3. On one side of the bag, trace or transfer the template provided (Figure 2). Place the image 2" (5.1cm) from the bottom and 2" (5.1cm) from the right side of the linen.

4. Before you begin embroidering place your stabilizer under the design and secure the corners with safety pins.

5. Embroider your design following the color/stitching guide. Once finished, tear off the excess stabilizer from around the design.

fold up in half

2" (5.1cm) from right and bottom edges

Figure 2

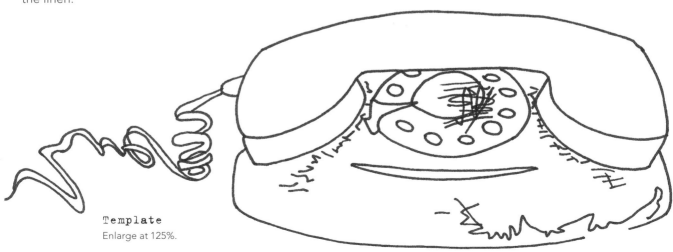

Template
Enlarge at 125%.

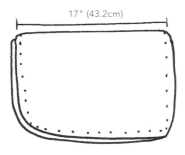

17" (43.2cm)

Figure 3

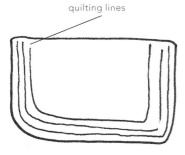

quilting lines

Figure 4

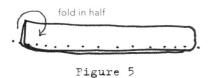

fold in half

Figure 5

fold up twice

Figure 6

Sewing and construction

1. First, construct the top flap using your 17" × 23" (43.2cm × 58.4cm) main print piece. Fold the piece in half, matching up the two 17" (43.2cm) sides (right sides together), and topstitch around the sides and bottom, leaving the top raw edge open (Figure 3).

2. Turn your piece right sides out and press. Place your small piece of fusible fleece in between the fabric and iron it in place. If it is bunchy, you may need to trim it a bit.

3. Quilt a few lines around the three sewn edges. I used four lines, ¼" (6mm) apart (Figure 4).

4. Next, construct the straps. Your two 4" × 36" (10.2cm × 91.4cm) pieces will each become a strap. Fold each piece in half lengthwise (right sides together) and sew down the side (Figure 5).

5. Turn each strap right side out and press so that the seam is centered on the back. Fold one end over twice, ½" (13mm) for each fold, and sew in place (Figure 6). Repeat for the other strap.

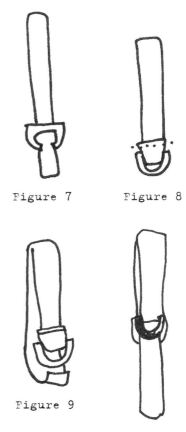

Figure 7

Figure 8

Figure 9

Figure 10

6. Slide the sewn end of one strap through two of your D-rings (Figure 7). Fold the sewn end over both rings and sew in place (Figure 8). Pass the unfinished edge of the strap through both rings from the back (Figure 9). Loop over the top ring and under the back ring and pull to secure (Figure 10). Repeat for the second strap.

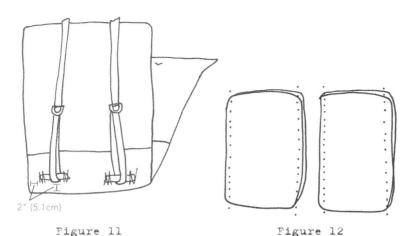

Figure 11

2" (5.1cm)

Figure 12

front side of flap
facing bag

right side
of straps
facing bag

back of
right side
of bag

Figure 13

7. Set your straps aside for now. Iron your fusible fleece to the wrong side of the outside bag piece and also to the 17" × 41½" (43.2cm × 105.4cm) white linen piece (this will be your lining).

8. Fold the outside piece in half again—this time with right sides together—and press to regain your fold line.

9. Place each strap on the outside of the bag. Flip your outside piece so the side without the embroidery is facing you. Place the loop end of the strap at the bottom of the bag, 2" (5.1cm) up from the fold on the white linen and 2" (5.1cm) from the side. Pin in place.

10. Place a 4" (10.2cm) piece of cording through each strap loop. Secure each end of cording with a big zigzagged line (Figure 11). Be sure to only secure the cording ends and do not catch the strap loop. Repeat for the second strap.

11. Fold your outside bag piece so that the right sides are together and sew a seam up both sides, leaving only the top open. Be sure to secure the ends. Repeat for your lining piece (Figure 12).

12. Next, line up the raw edge of the flap, the top of the straps and the top of the back of the bag (Figure 13). The straps will be in between the flap and the bag. Pin in place.

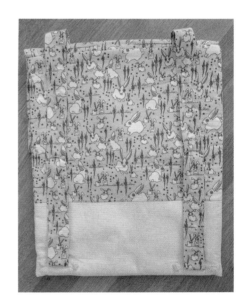

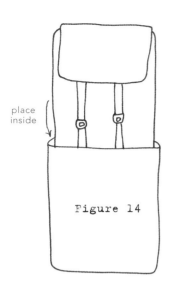

place inside

Figure 14

13. Now place the outside of the bag (along with the pinned flap and straps) in the inside of the lining piece (Figure 14). The lining of the bag will be turned inside out so that the right sides will be facing each other.

14. Pin and sew around the top opening, leaving an 8" (20.3cm) opening in the front (Figure 15). You may have to use a deeper seam here in order to catch all layers.

15. Once sewn, pull the inside out and push the lining down into the bag. Push out all corners and press. Slip stitch the opening closed (Figure 16).

16. Cut a piece of 90" (228.6cm) cording. Fold over at 25" (63.5cm) and place on the center of the flap. Sew in place with a few zigzagged lines (Figure 17). Tie a knot at each end of the cording to keep it from unraveling.

17. Finally, pull the long piece of cord around the bottom of the bag and over the top, meeting the shorter piece at the end of the flap, and tie in a bow to close the bag (Figure 18).

Figure 15

Figure 16

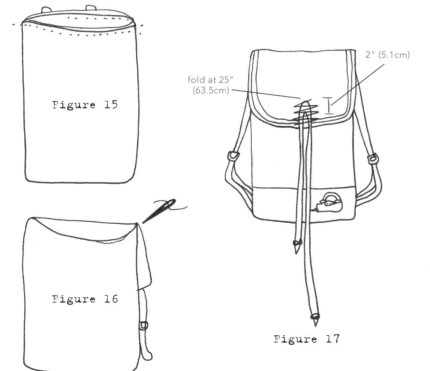

fold at 25" (63.5cm)

2" (5.1cm)

Figure 17

Figure 18

Index

Appliqué, 12, 28, 32, 43, 51, 74, 88, 92, 106, 112, 116–117

Backstitch, 8, 23, 50, 75, 80, 81, 113, 120
Backwards work, tracing and appliquéing, 112
Batting, 60
Binding, 13, 46, 74, 102, 117
Blanket stitch, 8, 32, 43, 50, 51, 88, 92, 106, 113
Borders
    calculating length, 45
    cutting, 42
Buttonhole, 107
Buttons, lining up and attaching, 109

Circles, cutting, 106
Corners, rounding, 32
Couched filling stitch, 9, 84

Designs
    repetition, 18
    tracing and transfer-ring, 12, 18, 22, 27, 32, 36, 43, 50, 54, 64, 74, 102, 112, 121
    working with back-wards, 112
Dyeing, 36

Embroidery
    keeping back neat, 6
    See also Appliqué, Stitches
Experimentation, 7

Fabrics, 6
Felted wool, 106
Floss, 6, 7
Flower guide, 93
Framing, 23, 79
"Frankenstein" stitches, 116–117
French knot, 9, 50, 54, 80, 81
Fusible fleece, 7, 56, 64, 84, 106, 122, 123
Fusible web, 7, 32, 43, 51, 88, 92, 106, 112, 116

Grid, 84

Handles, constructing, 66
Hoops, 6

Ironing, 6, 23, 123
    patches, 88
    with 360 E-Z Stitch, 23, 78

Lazy daisy stitch, 9, 92
Lining, 57, 66–67, 124

Marking cross stitch, 8, 33

Needle-turn appliqué, 12, 74

Panels, quilt, 42–43
Pearl cotton, 7
Piecing, 42, 72–73, 99–100, 120–121
Piping, 107–108
Plate, for rounding edges, 32, 106

Quilting, 12–13, 27, 32, 46, 74, 102, 117

Raw-edge appliqué, 12, 28
Running stitch, 8, 60, 80, 81, 102, 113

Sashing, 42, 43
Satin stitch, 6, 23, 27, 50, 54, 65, 75, 80, 81, 102, 113, 120
Scraps, saving, 72
Shrinkage, 102
Single buttonhole bar stitch, 9, 107
Single stitch, 120
Skein, 7
    unrolling and cutting, 10

Slip stitch, 9, 57, 67, 107
Stitches, 8–11
Strand, 7
Straps, constructing, 122
Supplies, basic, 7

360 E-Z Stitch, 6, 22–23, 27, 54, 64, 74, 78, 102, 121
Top stitching, 78
Tracing, 12, 18, 22, 27, 36, 43, 50, 54, 64, 74, 78, 84, 102, 112, 121
Transferring, 12, 27, 36, 43, 50, 102, 112, 121
Triangles, cutting, 72, 98
Twilling, 10–11, 18, 64–65

Washing instructions, 6–7
Whipped running stitch, 8, 43, 102
WOF, 7
Wrap 'n Fuse piping, 107

Zigzagged stitches, 123, 124
Zipper, attaching, 56

17 16 15 14 13   5 4 3 2 1

DISTRIBUTED IN CANADA BY FRASER DIRECT
100 Armstrong Avenue
Georgetown, ON, Canada L7G 5S4
Tel: (905) 877-4411

DISTRIBUTED IN THE U.K. AND EUROPE BY F+W MEDIA INTERNATIONAL
Brunel House, Newton Abbot, Devon, TQ12 4PU, England
Tel: (+44) 1626 323200, Fax: (+44) 1626 323319
Email: postmaster@davidandcharles.co.uk

DISTRIBUTED IN AUSTRALIA BY CAPRICORN LINK
P.O. Box 704, S. Windsor NSW, 2756 Australia
Tel: (02) 4560 1600, Fax: (02) 4577 5288
Email: books@capricornlink.com.au

ISBN-13: 978-1-4402-3558-0
ISBN-10: 1-4402-3558-9
SRN: U2915

www.fwmedia.com

Edited by *Stefanie Laufersweiler and Roseann Biederman*

Designed by *Julie Barnett*

Photography by *Corrie Schaffeld*

Styling by *Lauren Siedentopf*

Illustrations by *Megan Frock*

Production coordinated by *Greg Nock*

Special thanks to the Mellin family for graciously providing their home as a setting for many of the photos.

Metric Conversion Chart		
TO CONVERT	TO	MULTIPLY BY
inches	centimeters	2.54
centimeters	inches	0.4
feet	centimeters	30.5
centimeters	feet	0.03
yards	meters	0.9
meters	yards	1.1

Projects have been designed and created using imperial measurements and, although metric measurements have been provided, it is important to stick to using either imperial or metric throughout as discrepancies can occur.

About the author

Photo by Cindy Harper

As a southern gal who longs for all things urban, Megan Frock's design style reflects just that: a brilliant mixture of urban, modern and vintage all rolled up in a sweet southern package. Megan's passion for all things crafty began at age 7 when her father taught her to crochet a single chain stitch. She was constantly wanting more, entering coloring contests and constructing anything she could with a hot glue gun. Megan went on to pursue her passion as she entered college, majoring in mixed media painting. After college, Megan worked as a freelance painter, showing work everywhere from rural Arkansas galleries to the Visual Arts Center of New Jersey.

After many years Megan decided to give her tattered paintbrushes a break and pull out her sewing machine. Since then, she has dived head first into sewing and creating. Known to the sewing industry as Downtown Housewife, Megan portrays just that: a housewife with a passion, proving to women everywhere that sewing should be a part of everyday life. Follow Megan on Twitter (@MeganFrock) and Facebook or Instagram (both @DowntownHousewife).

Acknowledgments

Thank you to the following resources:

Sew Sweet Quilt Shop in Brunswick, Missouri, for supplying me with the best fabric, notions and support.

Jessica Defibaugh, for her excellent machine quilting skills.

Tula Pink, for answering every idiotic question I have had, even if it was 1 a.m.

My patient husband, Jimmy, who ate leftovers more than he would have liked.

The F+W team, for simply believing in me.

Cindy Harper of Cindy Harper Photography in Tina, Missouri, for my author photo.

Dedication

This book is dedicated to my Grandma Bobbie, for teaching me how to sew, crochet and embroider at the ripe age of 7. She unintentionally gave me my love for hand stitching. I wasn't allowed to use her shiny black Singer. To this day, I can recall staring desperately through the door of her sewing room and thinking to myself, "How does that work? Is it fast? And can it cut my finger off?" I can recall numerous occasions when I thought that if I could sneak in fast enough, I could use it. Somehow, the fear of cutting my finger off, and even worse, the fear of my grandma fetching a switch, kept me from entering. It wasn't until I was 23 that I got my first sewing machine, and since then I have learned two things: It would be nearly impossible to lose a finger, and I still prefer to hand stitch.

Keep on stitching and sewing!

Visit **store.MarthaPullen.com** for all the fabrics, threads, tools and notions you need, and check out these exciting titles for valuable instruction and endless inspiration.

Celebrate with a Stitch

Over 20 Gorgeous Sewing, Stitching and Embroidery Projects for Every Occasion

Mandy Shaw

Celebrate births, birthdays, weddings, Christmas and other celebrations in style, with stitching! Mandy Shaw's "folksy" style combined with retro and vintage fabrics and colorways appeal to sewists of all ages. The pretty decorations you create with Mandy's easy step-by-step instruction are sure to be a hit at your next party.

A Sewn Vintage Lifestyle

20 Pieced and Appliquéd Projects for Quilts, Bags and More

Verna Mosquera

Sew beautiful projects you'll love to use! Create 20 charming projects perfect for your lifestyle using patchwork, appliqué and embroidery techniques, all illustrated by pattern and fabric designer Verna Mosquera. Let Verna guide you through the process and projects so you can start creating a handmade lifestyle all your own!